CHINESE
COOKERY SECRETS

Deh-Ta Hsiung was born in Beijing and travelled widely throughout China as a teenager. Coming from a family of gourmets and scholars, his interest in food and wine developed as he grew up in a traditional classical Chinese upbringing. Deh-Ta came to England in 1950 to complete his education at Oxford and London. He is an acknowledged expert on Chinese food and cookery, besides being the author of several bestselling books and a food and wine consultant for Chinese restaurants and food manufacturers. He is also a tutor of international renown – he was a regular teacher at the late Ken Lo's Chinese Cookery School in London between 1981 and 1996, and he taught in many other institutes all over the UK and at the Ballymaloe Cookery School in County Cork, Ireland on several occasions, as well as in France, Italy, Finland and as far away as India, where he was sent by the UN to conduct several courses in the country's leading catering institutes.

Several of Deh-Ta's books have been translated into all the major European languages and the German edition of *The Chinese Kitchen* (*Die Chinesische Küche*) was awarded a silver medal by the Gastronomische Akademie Deutschlands in 2001.

CHINESE COOKERY SECRETS

How To Cook Chinese Restaurant Food At Home

Deh-Ta Hsiung

RIGHT WAY

Constable & Robinson Ltd
3 The Lanchesters
162 Fulham Palace Road
London W6 9ER
www.constablerobinson.com

First published in the UK 1993

This new edition published by Right Way,
an imprint of Constable & Robinson, 2009

Copyright © Deh-Ta Hsiung, 1993, 2009

3

The right of Deh-Ta Hsiung to be identified as the author of this
work has been asserted by him in accordance with the Copyright,
Designs & Patents Act, 1988.

A copy of the British Library Cataloguing in Publication Data is
available from the British Library

ISBN: 978-0-7160-2224-4

Printed and bound in the EU

CONTENTS

To Thelma, Kai-Lu, Anna and Benjamin

FOREWORD

If you have always wanted to try cooking Chinese food at home, but have been put off by the daunting thought of following recipes with intricate preparations and complicated cooking techniques; or your attempts have somehow never quite managed to achieve that subtle flavour and delicate texture which are the hallmarks of authentic Chinese cooking, then this book will, for the first time, reveal to you the simple 'secrets' of the Chinese kitchen.

First of all, not everyone realises that there is a world of difference between food produced by the commercial establishments and that of the ordinary homes in China. This is not just because of a difference in skills between the professional chefs and the home cooks, but more a matter of a difference in the *style of cooking* based on resources and facilities which are strikingly varied between a restaurant and a home kitchen.

Secondly, almost all the Chinese cookbooks in English have been written by people who have little or no knowledge of a Chinese *restaurant* kitchen; they usually contain recipes drastically modified in order to accommodate the average home cook in the West, and often with misleading instructions for the various cooking techniques, or inaccurate explanations of the use of special ingredients and seasonings. No wonder so many would-be Chinese cooks have been disappointed and frustrated by their attempts to produce their favourite restaurant dishes at home.

I have been involved with Chinese cookery since early childhood, as I first learnt cooking from my mother and the family cook in China. Later on, I took lessons 'from some of the leading Chinese chefs in England and Hong Kong, and have since spent a great deal of time in many restaurants in different parts of the world. I have also over twelve years' worldwide teaching experience of Chinese cookery to home cooks as well as to professionals – and so I have a deep understanding of the obstacles that prevent anyone from producing Chinese dishes of restaurant quality at home.

Fortunately, very few of the 'obstacles' are insurmountable, and with the help of this book, it is my sincere hope that you will be able to achieve that subtle flavour and delicate texture that have been eluding you up until now.

In the early days of inter-change between the East and the West, very few linguists were specialists in all the different fields (least of all on food and cooking). So once an English definition of a Chinese food or cooking method was struck upon, it was passed down in common usage and became established as fact, however inaccurate the original translation might have been. I have therefore inserted Chinese names for all the recipe names given in this book.

The recipes are arranged in groups according to the various cooking methods rather than the main ingredients, unlike the normal practice in a restaurant menu and in Western cookbooks. My main reason for breaking this convention is to avoid the tedium of too much unnecessary repetition of step-by-step cooking instructions for each individual recipe.

I have also allocated to each group of recipes a percentage mark for the feasibility of attaining a superb restaurant quality. Given the skills of the cook and the facilities available, one could expect, say, a 95%–100% success rate for certain dishes, but only 85%–90% for others.

Obviously different restaurants produce different food, and each chef has his specialties – it would be very boring to eat dishes tasting identical time after time, however good they are. So forget that particular delicious dish you had in the 'Green Dragon' last week, and aim to achieve your own individual mark. If it tastes good to you, and other people enjoy it as well, then you have succeeded and you can give yourself a 99%, if not a 100%, mark!

Deh-Ta Hsiung

熊徳達

SHOPPING GUIDE

There are a great number of Chinese provision stores throughout the British Isles. In the larger cities they usually centre around a district known as Chinatown. They do warrant a special visit if you happen to be living near one of them: it is quite an experience as you feel as if you are entering a different world – with all the exotic smells and packagings. Most of these stores are open seven days a week, sometimes well into late evenings. You can also buy online from established stores such as Wing Yip (www.wingyipstore.co.uk) and Hoo Hing (www.hoohing.com).

The following is a selected list of Chinese provision stores.

Birmingham
Wing Yip, 375 Nechells Park Road, Nechells, Birmingham,
   B7 5NT.

Edinburgh
Pat's Chung Ying, 199 Leith Walk, Edinburgh, EH6 8NX
   (www.patschungying.co.uk).

Leeds
Wing Lee Hong (www.wingleehong.co.uk).

London
Loon Fung, 4 stores (www.loonfung.com).
Loon Moon, 9 Gerrard Street, London, WID 5PN.
Wing Yip, 395 Edgware Road, Cricklewood, London, NW2 6LN.
Wing Yip, 544 Purley Way, Croydon, CRO 4NZ.

Manchester
Wing Fat, 49 Faulkner Street, Manchester, MI 4EE
   (www.wingfat.co.uk).
Wing Yip, Oldham Road, Ancoats, Manchester, M4 5HU.

Oxford
Lung Wah Chong, Lung Wah House, Osney Mead, Oxford,
   OX2 OES (www.lungwahchong.com).

INTRODUCTION

A certain 'uniqueness' distinguishes Chinese cooking from all other food cultures – perhaps with the exception of South-East Asia – not only in the preparation and cooking, but also in the serving and eating of the food, so I urge you to read this short Introduction very carefully and to study the following two sections on equipment and preparation thoroughly before trying out any recipes. I've deliberately left Menu Planning to the end, so that you can try out just one or two dishes first, before going for a full-scale meal.

The Principles of Chinese Cooking

The main distinctive feature of Chinese cooking is the emphasis on the harmonious blending of **colour**, **aroma**, **flavour** and **shape**, both in a single dish and in a course of dishes.

The principle of blending complementary or contrasting colours and flavours is a fundamental one: the different ingredients must not be mixed indiscriminately; the blending of different flavours is controlled and should follow a set pattern. The cutting of ingredients is another important element in Chinese cooking: in order to achieve the proper effect, slices are matched with slices, shreds with shreds, cubes with cubes, chunks with chunks, and so on. This is not only for the sake of appearance, but also because ingredients of the same size and shape require about the same amount of time in cooking.

This complexity of inter-related elements of colours, aromas, flavours and shapes is reinforced by another feature: **texture**. A dish may have just one, or several contrasting textures – such as tenderness, crispiness, crunchiness, smoothness and softness. The textures to be avoided are: sogginess, stringiness and hardness. The selection of different textures in one single dish is an integral part of the blending of different flavours and colours.

The desired texture or textures in any dish can only be achieved by the right cooking methods. The size and shape of the cut ingredient must, first of all, be suitable for the particular method of cooking. For instance, ingredients for quick stir-frying should be cut into small, thin slices or shreds, never large, thick chunks.

In all the different methods of cooking, the correct cooking time and degree of heat are of vital importance. Learn and understand the character of the ingredients (their textures and their colour changes) – an important factor that determines the appropriate cutting and cooking methods.

A Chinese dish is usually made up of more than one ingredient, because when a single item is served on its own it lacks contrast and therefore harmony. For centuries, Chinese cooks have understood the importance of the harmonious balance in blending different flavours.

Without going too deeply into the realm of Chinese philosophy, I would just like to mention the ancient school of thought known as *yin-yang*, which practically governs all aspects of the Chinese way of life, and has been the guiding principle for all Chinese cooks.

Consciously or unconsciously, every Chinese cook from the housewife to the professional chef, works to the *yin-yang* principles – i.e. the harmonious balance and contrast in conspicuous juxtaposition of different colours, aromas, flavours and textures by varying the ingredients, cutting techniques, seasonings and cooking methods.

Perhaps one of the best examples of the *yin-yang* principle in Chinese cooking is in the way we blend different seasonings in complementary pairs: sugar *(yin)* with vinegar *(yang)*; salt *(yin)* with pepper *(yang)*; spring onion *(yin)* with ginger *(yang)*; soy sauce *(yin)* with wine *(yang)* and so on.

The 'Secrets' of the Chinese Kitchen

You must have wondered, when visiting a Chinese restaurant, how it is that you never have to wait long before several dishes, all freshly cooked and piping hot, appear at your table (or for take-away) from a menu listing well over one hundred items.

The secret is all in the preliminary preparations before the actual cooking. As you will see from the detailed instructions for each recipe in this book, the preparation for most dishes takes up far more time than the final cooking time, which often requires no more than a couple of minutes to complete. I shall explain:

Take an average-sized Chinese restaurant, say with sixty to seventy seatings. There is usually a staff of six or seven working in the kitchen (the waiting staff can be anything from three to eight, depending on the locality of the establishment), most of them working on a ten–twelve hour shift, six days a week.

The general routine is as follows: at 10 am each day, the staff start to arrive, and fresh supplies of ingredients are delivered. These have to be given whatever preliminary preparation is necessary.

One of the first tasks is to make the stock (see page 45), which is used as a basis for soup, as well as for general cooking whenever liquid is required. Then the prawns have to be peeled and the meat cut into slices, shreds or cubes, and marinated. Ducks and chickens are prepared for cooking, and vegetables are cut into various sizes and shapes.

The staff have their lunch as early as 11.30 or 11.45 in order to be ready for the opening at noon. When an order comes through, the chef or his assistant doles out the exact amount of pre-prepared ingredients on separate dishes and places them on the work top just behind the stove by which the chef and one or two cooks are stationed, with woks and oils pre-heated to the required temperature, ready for action.

The gas cookers have been converted to give extremely high heat, so thinly cut meat like pork and beef can be cooked in one and a half minutes, while chicken and fish can often take less than half that time.

During the rush hours, a chef can operate two woks side by side simultaneously, which means that three cooks can turn out six quick stir-fried dishes in two minutes flat! Apart from the soy-braised and roasted food, almost every item on the menu is freshly cooked from pre-prepared ingredients. Some dishes may partly contain pre-cooked items, but certainly not to the same extent as the mass-produced dishes from a cheap Chinese take-away.

You will probably have noticed the difference between the food you get in a restaurant of good standing and that from a cheap take-away. The dishes from the former are always bright, crisp and crunchy as well as delicious, while the food from the latter is usually dull, soggy and often without much flavour.

This apparent discrepancy of quality between restaurants and take-away food is a question of resources. Almost all the small take-aways are run by families which usually consist of the father as cook, the mother as the kitchen hand, and the son and/or daughter as the cashier and general helper. They may list some fifty to sixty items on the menu, but on closer scrutiny you will discover that more than half of the dishes are variations of the same thing. They almost all consist of the ubiquitous bean sprouts, plus two or three other shredded vegetables (usually carrot and onion), with a small amount of meat or prawns; furthermore, nearly all the ingredients are pre-cooked so it is merely a matter of assembling everything together and warming them through at the last minute.

Should you wish to reproduce your favourite Chinese dishes at home, you should have no difficulty in matching or even surpassing the standard of a good take-away; however, in matching the food from a restaurant of high quality, I must warn you not to set your expectations too high, bearing in mind not only the differences in facilities between a professional Chinese kitchen and an average British home kitchen, but also the years of training and experience of the chefs.

But all is not lost. While there are a number of dishes that are beyond the scope of the home cook in a home kitchen, a large number of the most popular dishes can be produced successfully at home by following the instructions in this book.

If your first attempt at a Chinese meal from this book turns out to be a triumph – or even a modest success – I take off my hat to you and say: 'Well done!', and congratulate both of us. But if the results are not quite as good as you expected, don't be down-hearted and give up. Remember the mottoes: 'If at first you don't succeed, try, try, try again' and 'Practice makes perfect'. Try and find out where you have gone wrong and then you'll no doubt be more successful the next time.

Bon appetit! – or *qing, qing!* as we say in China.

1

ESSENTIAL EQUIPMENT

The Chinese *batterie de cuisine* consists of very few basic implements: it is said that an itinerant Chinese chef carries only two pieces of equipment with him – a cleaver and a wok.

Opinions differ as to which Chinese equipment is essential in order to cook authentic Chinese food. Almost everyone agrees that besides the Chinese **cleaver** and the **wok**, four or five more items should be included: i.e. **chopping block**, **spatula** and/or **ladle**, **strainer** and **steamer**.

In a Western kitchen, equivalent equipment is always available: cutting knives and board, pots and frying-pans, fish slices and stirrers, sieves and strainers, and so on and so forth. But the Chinese cooking utensils are of ancient design, they are made of basic and inexpensive materials, and they have been in continuous use for several thousand years, each serving a special function.

Their more sophisticated and much more expensive Western counterparts prove rather inadequate in contrast, especially if you want to reproduce those wonderful dishes from your favourite Chinese restaurants and take-aways at home.

Obviously there is no need for you to rush out and buy every single item I have just mentioned. Try using your existing equipment first; but if you are not happy with the result, then you can go for the real thing.

Chinese Cleaver
A Chinese cleaver may appear to the uninitiated to be hefty and ominously sharp. But in reality it is quite light, steady and not at all dangerous to use, provided you handle it correctly and with care!

I think the term 'cleaver' is a mistranslation – its Chinese name should be rendered as 'kitchen knife'. Once you learn to regard it as a kitchen tool mainly used for cutting and *not* just a chopper, then you will be surprised how easy and simple it is to use compared with an expensive Western kitchen knife.

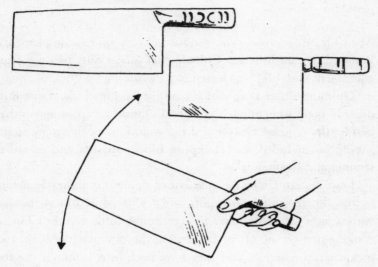

Fig. 1. Chinese cleavers.
Left: No. 1 cleaver.
Right: No. 2 cleaver.
Bottom: How to hold a cleaver.

Chinese cleavers are available in a variety of materials and weights. They usually come in three sizes. No. 1 being the heaviest with a blade about 23cm (9") long and 10cm (4") wide, it can weigh up to almost 1kg (or 2lb); it is really a chopper rather than a knife. No. 3 is much smaller and lighter, with the blade about 20cm (8") long and 8cm (3") wide, with less than half of the weight of No. 1 – it is sometimes called a slicer.

But the much preferred knife by everyone is the medium-weight, dual-purpose No. 2, also known as *wen-wu dao* (civil and military knife). You use the lighter, front half of the blade for slicing, shredding and scoring, etc; and the heavier, rear half of the blade for chopping and so on. You can also use the back of the blade as a pounder and tenderizer, and the flat side of the blade for crushing and transporting; while the end of the handle can even be used as a pestle for grinding spices.

When buying a cleaver, hold it in your hand and feel the weight; choose one that is neither too heavy nor too light. The ones made of carbonized steel with a wooden handle are generally heavier than the ones made of stainless steel with either metal or wooden handles. While a stainless steel cleaver may look good, it requires more frequent sharpening in order to keep the cutting edge razor-sharp. To prevent the carbonized steel blade getting stained and rusting, wipe it dry after use, then give it a thin coating of vegetable oil.

Sharpen the cleaver on a fine-grained whetstone, honing the blade evenly on both sides to keep it straight and sharp. Hang the cleaver by the handle to keep the blade from becoming dulled on other metal objects in a drawer.

Chopping Block
The traditional Chinese chopping block is a cross-section of a tree trunk. Made of hardwood, they range from about 25cm (10") in diameter and 4cm (1^1/$_2$") thick, to giant ones up to 50cm (20") by 15–20cm (6–8"). The ideal size for a home kitchen should be about 30cm (12") in diameter and at least 5cm (2") thick to be of any real use.

To prevent it from splitting, season a new block with a liberal dose of vegetable oil on both sides. Let the wood absorb as much oil as it will take, then sponge the block with salt and water and dry it thoroughly. Never soak the block in water nor wash it with any detergent – after each use, just scrape it clean with the blade of your cleaver, then wipe the surface with a sponge or cloth wrung out in plain hot water. Always stand the block on its side when not in use to prevent it from warping.

Nowadays it is possible to obtain split-free wood block, as well as plastic chopping board made of white acrylic, which will not split, smell or warp. But they lack the aesthetic appeal of a traditional tree trunk with its beautiful pattern of grains.

If you already have a large, rectangular board of hard wood, at least 5cm (2") thick, then it should take the heaviest blows from a cleaver. Use one side for chopping only, then the other side should remain smooth enough for general cutting, or even for pastry-making.

The Wok

The Chinese cooking utensil known as the *wok* derives its name from the Cantonese for 'pot' or 'pan'; the correct transliteration should be *guo*. But wok it is, and wok it shall remain – as with the Chinese 'cleaver'. I will show you several more misinterpretations throughout the book, but in most cases I will just have to give up the struggle and use the conventional and the customary names in order not to confuse the issue!

The wok was designed with a rounded bottom to fit snugly over a traditional Chinese brazier or stove, which burns wood, charcoal or coke. It conducts and retains heat evenly, and because of the wok's shape, the food always returns to the centre where the heat is most intense.

Of course the wok is far more versatile than just a frying-pan: it is also used for deep-frying, braising, steaming, boiling, and even smoking – in other words, the whole spectrum of Chinese cooking methods can be executed in one single utensil.

Despite the ever-increasing popularity of Chinese cooking all over the world, the average non-Chinese still cannot quite come to terms with the use of the wok, and most people just seem not to be able to grasp the few fundamentals that make this utensil stand apart from all other kitchen equipment in the West. I think the explanation for this is quite simple: since the wok was originally designed to be used over a primitive stove, its rounded bottom is not really suitable for a modern Western cooker, particularly if you cook only by electricity.

Basically, there are only two different types of wok on the market. First, there is the wok with two handles at opposite sides, usually sold as a set with the adaptor ring, lid, ladle, spatula, steamer rack and other accessories. Then, for less than a third of the price, you can buy a wok with a single handle like that of a frying-pan.

Let us take a look at the double-handled wok first. It is usually made of lightweight carbonized steel, and the diameter ranges from 28cm (11") to 32cm (12½"). Some makes have a slightly flattened bottom specially designed for electric cookers, but they can also be used on all other cookers; while the traditional rounded bottom wok needs an adaptor ring or hob stand, unless you have a gas cooker with burners that will cradle the rounded bottom. The double-handled wok is ideal for deep-frying, braising, boiling and steaming, but is not really suitable for quick stir-frying as you need a strong wrist to lift and shake it about, and also the handles get very hot even if they are insulated with plastic or wood.

Fig. 2. Double-handled woks.
Left: Round bottomed wok.
Right: Flat bottomed wok.

The single-handled wok is much preferred by the professionals. It may appear to be unsteady and slightly tipped to one side, but in fact it is quite safe and much easier to handle. There is never any real danger of the whole wok tipping over as the sheer weight of the wok and of the ingredients inside help to balance it. Again, a slightly flattened version is available for electric cookers.

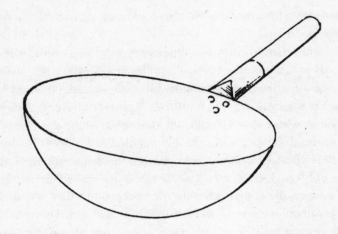

Fig. 3. Single-handled wok.

Woks made from stainless steel, aluminium, copper, Teflon, porcelainized enamel, with coloured exterior and so on are specifically designed and manufactured for the Western home kitchen. However, not only do they always cost a great deal more than the traditional iron or steel wok, but they are also far less efficient for the task they are supposed to perform.

In order to produce a whole range of dishes of restaurant standard, the ideal wok would be a single-handled one made of medium-weight carbonized steel, with a diameter of 33cm (13"), and not less than 10cm (4") deep. The depth of the wok is quite important: the extra inch or so on its vertical wall will make your cooking that much easier and more successful, particularly for stir-frying.

A double-handled wok made of lightweight carbonized steel would be useful as your second wok, to be used for braising, deep-frying, boiling and steaming, etc. But not many cookers are big enough to accommodate two woks at the same time, so you might find an electric wok (extremely expensive) very useful as it frees your cooker for other use.

How to season and clean a wok

A new iron or steel wok is coated either with machine oil or a film of wax to keep it from rusting. Before use, this coating must be removed and then a new coat of seasoning applied to the surface. This 'seasoning' must be maintained throughout the life of the wok to keep it from rusting, and to prevent food sticking to the bottom.

The best way to remove the oil or wax coating of a new wok is by burning: heat the wok over a hot stove until almost the entire surface is black, let it cool, then clean it in warm, soapy water with a stiff brush and rinse well. Place the wok over a moderate heat just to dry, then wipe the surface clean with a pad of kitchen paper soaked in cooking oil. The wok is now seasoned and ready for use.

After each use, wash the wok under the hot or cold water tap. *Never use detergents* as they will remove the 'seasoning' and food will stick to the surface the next time you cook. Should any food be left sticking to the wok, scrape it off with a stiff brush or nylon scourer – don't use soap. Rinse and dry the wok thoroughly over a low heat. If the wok is not to be used again soon, rub some oil over the surface to prevent it going rusty.

When you have cooked in a new wok some eight to ten times, and if you never clean it with detergents or metal abrasives, then it will acquire a beautiful, glossy finish like a well-seasoned omelette pan. This patina is much treasured by Chinese cooks as it creates the 'wok flavour'.

Chinese Spatula and Ladle

Some wok sets consist of a pair of stirrers in the shape of a spatula and a ladle, made of iron or stainless steel, each with a long metal handle and a wooden tip.

Fig. 4. Ladle.

Of the two, the ladle or scooper is more versatile. It is really a miniature wok with a long handle (its Chinese name actually means a little wok), and is an indispensable utensil in the professional kitchen, since it is used for adding ingredients and seasonings to the wok besides being a stirrer and scooper during cooking, as well as for transferring cooked food from the wok to a serving dish or bowl.

It is also a measurer for the cook: a standard-size ladle will hold about 175ml (6 fluid oz) liquid, slightly smaller than a rice bowl.

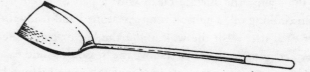

Fig. 5. Chinese spatula.

The spatula or shovel has a rounded end to match the contours of the wok, therefore it can be very useful for scraping and lifting food from the bottom of the wok such as when cooking a whole fish, or large, thin slices of food.

One common factor regarding the wooden tip attached at the end of the metal handle: it often becomes loose and falls off in your hand during cooking! So make sure it is nailed or glued firmly in place – you may have to do this yourself, since very seldom will you find this has been done by the manufacturers.

Strainers

There are two types of strainer used in a Chinese kitchen: one is made of copper or steel wire with a long bamboo handle (comparatively inexpensive); the other is made of perforated metal (iron or stainless steel, quite expensive). Strainers are used to scoop food out of hot oil or water. Their disc-like shape enables you to transfer large quantities of food quickly to avoid over-cooking.

Fig. 6. Strainers.

Steamers

Again, there are two types of steamer: the traditional one made of bamboo, very pretty but not so easy to track down; or the modern version made of aluminium, widely available. It is not always necessary to use a Chinese steamer for certain dishes as you can easily improvise with a rack or trivet and a dome-shaped lid with the wok. Full details will be found in the steaming section on page 109.

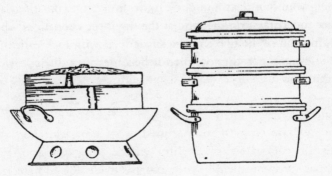

Fig. 7. Steamers.
Left: Traditional (bamboo) steamer.
Right: Modern (aluminium) steamer.

Chopsticks

You may well wonder whether chopsticks are essential for Chinese cooking: the answer is yes and no!

Basically, there are only two types of chopsticks available: the very long ones – up to 41cm (16") long, made of bamboo or wood; these are used for cooking only, rather like a pair of tongs. Then there are the standard-length chopsticks – between 25-28cm (10–11") long – made of bamboo, lacquered wood, or heat-resistant plastic. These are mainly used at the table, but they can also be very useful in the kitchen, such as for mixing (instead of using a fork or spoon), and for egg-beating (instead of using an egg whisk). So, it is not absolutely essential to have chopsticks in the kitchen.

When it comes to using chopsticks for eating, I think it *is* essential that you should have them at the table. This is not purely an aesthetic question, but also a practical point – partly because all Chinese food is prepared in such a way that it is easily picked up by chopsticks; also, since you can only pick up a small morsel at a time, you really have to chew the food well before swallowing it down, thus chopsticks help the digestion as well as increasing your appreciation of the flavour of the food.

Learning to use chopsticks is quite simple and easy – use fig. 8 to help you. Just relax and don't fix your eyes on your fingers, but rather concentrate on the food at the tip of the chopsticks – by the way, make sure the two chopsticks are level with each other, if the two sticks are not aligned, then it becomes very difficult to pick anything up.

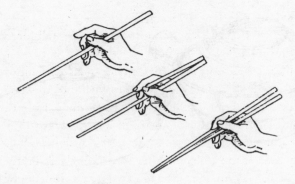

Fig. 8. How to hold chopsticks.

Chinese Casserole or Sand-Pot

Made of earthenware (hence the name sand-pot), casseroles as cooking utensils must have preceded metal ones by many thousands of years in China.

They come in a variety of shapes and sizes. The most common shape is a squat casserole with sloping sides, unglazed on the outside and glazed on the inside, with a flared, hollow handle and a snug-fitting lid which is often glazed dark brown on the outside. Some of the lids have two little loops through which a strand of string or wire can be threaded to make a handle. This type of casserole comes in sizes to serve one, two, four or many more.

The other type is also squat and has two handles. It has a smoother-textured exterior, but usually comes in large sizes only.

In China, earthenware casseroles are always used for stove-top cooking as they retain an overall even heat; they are ideal for braising and slow-cooking. Since they can be placed directly over gas or electric cookers, food cooked in a sand-pot requires much shorter cooking-time (thus using less fuel) than food placed in an oven.

Most sand-pots are rather fragile, so they do crack up easily; that's probably why some restaurants nowadays use a metal casserole made of stainless steel- not at all the same thing – such is a sign of the times!

Fig. 9. Sand-pots.

Obviously, it is not absolutely necessary to have a sand-pot in order to cook Chinese casseroles. Enamelled or cast-iron casseroles with lids can be used instead, provided they are flame-proof.

Iron-Plate

The iron-plate sizzled dish is a Chinese version of the Japanese *Teppanyaki* or *sukiyaki*.

In Japan and Japanese restaurants in the West, raw ingredients are cooked in front of you, on your table. But in Chinese restaurants, the food is pre-cooked in the kitchen, then either brought to your table sizzling on an iron-plate or, in some cases, brought to your table on an ordinary dish before being tipped on to a very hot iron-plate in front of you, thus making a sizzling noise.

In order to do this at home, all you need is an iron-plate or griddle on a wooden base; they come in a variety of sizes (and shapes), but are comparatively inexpensive.

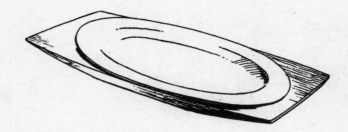

Fig. 10. **Iron-plate.**

2

INITIAL PREPARATION

I mentioned in the Introduction that there is a certain 'uniqueness' which distinguishes Chinese food from the Western world. Such a bold statement requires further qualification:

To start with, there is the Chinese division, when preparing and serving food, between *fan* (grains and other starch food) and *cai* (meat and vegetable dishes). Grains in the various forms of rice or wheat flour (bread, pancakes, noodles or dumplings, etc), make up the *fan* half of the meal. Vegetables and meats (including poultry and fish, etc), cut up and mixed in various combinations into individual dishes constitute the *cai* half. A balanced meal must have an appropriate amount of both *fan* and *cai*.

It is in the combining of various ingredients and the blending of different flavours for the preparation of *cai* that lie the fine art and skill of Chinese cooking. A Chinese cook abroad can always produce a Chinese meal, even using only local ingredients. For the 'Chineseness' of the food depends entirely on *how* it is prepared and cooked, not *what* ingredients are used.

Cutting Techniques

When describing the harmonious blending of colours, aromas, flavours, shapes and textures in the principles of Chinese cooking (see page 13), I also mentioned briefly about the importance of cutting.

The cutting of various ingredients into different sizes, thicknesses and shapes is an important element in Chinese cooking. The Chinese always cut their food into small, neat pieces before cooking, partly because of fuel conservation: small pieces of food can be cooked quickly before the sticks of firewood burn out; and partly because small pieces of food are easier to be served and eaten with chopsticks, since knives and carvers have never been used on Chinese tables. The fact that small pieces of food only require a short cooking time, thus retaining much of their natural flavours and nutritious value is an added bonus, which must be regarded as an incidental discovery – I know the Chinese are clever, but surely we couldn't have been that clever as far back as the Xia Dynasty in the 21st century BC!

So the Chinese started cutting their food into small pieces before cooking for practical reasons, but as their cuisine developed into a fine art, naturally the cutting too became more and more sophisticated. We must have found out the close relationship between cooking and cutting, so instead of cutting everything into small bits and pieces indiscriminately, we gradually worked out the following basic rules that govern cutting food:

1. The size and shape of the cut ingredient must, first of all, be suitable for the particular method of cooking. For instance, ingredients for quick stir-frying should be cut into small, thin slices or shreds, never large, thick chunks.

2. Learn and understand the character of the ingredients: their texture and their colour changes – an important factor that determines the appropriate cutting and cooking method. Tender ingredients can be cut thicker than tougher ones that require more cooking time; and most meats change colour when cooked (chicken and pork become paler, while beef and lamb tend to go darker after being cooked).

3. The ingredient must be cut into pieces of uniform shape, size and thickness. This is not only to create aesthetic harmony, but because each piece must be cooked evenly – larger pieces will otherwise be under cooked and smaller ones overcooked.

4. Whenever possible, different ingredients for the same dish should be cut into pieces of the same shape *and* size – slices are matched with slices, shreds with shreds, cubes with cubes, chunks with chunks and so on.

There are certain shapes which are standard in Chinese cooking: slice, strip, shred, chunk, piece, dice, cube, grain and mince. The actual shape is decided by the character of the ingredient and the cooking method required.

Fig. 11. To cut into slices.

SLICE: slices are thin, flat pieces of the ingredient.

First, cut the ingredient into sections as required by the dimension of the slices.

Then, slice the sections according to the desired thickness.

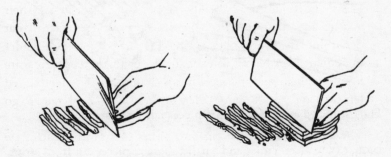

Fig. 12. To cut into strips (left) and shreds (right).

STRIP, SHRED: strips and shreds are similar – one is thicker, the other is thinner.

For strips: first, cut the ingredient into thick slices, then cut them into strips.

For shreds: first, cut the ingredient into thin slices, then pile them on top of each other like a pack of playing cards, and cut them into shreds.

Fig. 13. To cut into chunks and pieces.

CHUNK, PIECE: there are many kinds of chunks and pieces – diamond, hexagonal, rectangular or wedge-shaped.

First, cut the ingredient into broad strips or sections, then cut into smaller pieces as required.

Fig.14. Diced cubes (right) are pieces cut from strips (left).

DICE, CUBE: diced cubes and small cubes are pieces cut from strips.

Fig. 15. To chop into grains (left) and mince (right).

GRAIN, MINCE: grains are finely chopped ingredient, cut from shreds. Mince is even finer, and is cut by much chopping and pounding with the back of the cleaver.

In addition to these, there are FLOWER-CUTTING and SCORING for thick pieces of ingredient such as kidney, squid and fish. These cutting methods allow more heat and seasoning penetration. Details will be given with the appropriate recipes.

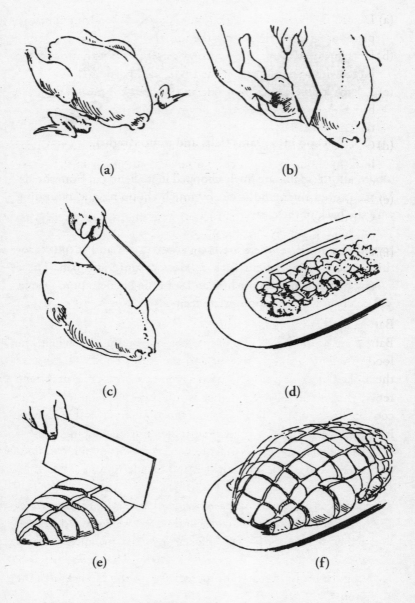

(a)

(b)

(c)

(d)

(e)

(f)

Fig. 16. Chopping up a whole chicken or duck for serving.

(a) Detach the two wings at the joints, then cut each wing into two pieces at its joint, discarding the tips.

(b) Detach the two thighs by cutting through the skin around the joints with a sharp knife or the tip of the cleaver.

(c) Lay the limbless bird on its side and separate the breasts from the backbone section by cutting down through the soft bone from the tail to neck.

(d) Carve away the skin and meat from the backbone section, cut into small bite-size pieces and arrange them neatly in the centre of an oval serving platter.

(e) Remove the wishbone as well as the main breastbone by hand. Cut the two breasts in half lengthwise, then chop each breast crosswise into neat small pieces.

(f) Chop the legs and thighs crosswise into small bite-size pieces and arrange them on each side of the breasts. Place the two wings on the upper part.

Batters and Thickening Agent

Batters are used to coat ingredients before cooking. They help the food to retain freshness, flavour and moisture. They will also give the cooked food a crisp outside and a tender, soft inside. Batters help retain the nutrients in food that would otherwise be lost in the cooking process. Finally, batters help the food retain its shape where it might have been broken up or shrunken during cooking.

The primary ingredients in batters are: egg, wheat flour, cornflour paste (see overleaf), baking powder, and breadcrumbs.

Thickening Agent is a thin paste made of starch (cornflour, water chestnut flour or potato flour, etc) and water. When added to food shortly before it is done it will thicken the gravy or sauce. It serves to:

1. Bring the seasonings and the ingredients together to heighten the flavours.

2. Make the surface of the cooked dish smooth and soft, and make

the colour bright – in other words, it improves the appearance of the dish.

3. Create a transparent coating around the food, keeping the heat in the food so that it doesn't get cold too quickly.

4. As in some soup dishes heavier ingredients tend to sink to the bottom, the thickening agent makes the ingredients remain more evenly distributed in the soup.

The commonest thickening agent used particularly in Chinese restaurants is **Cornflour Paste**. There are two types: *Thick paste* is made by mixing 1 part cornflour with about 1.2 parts of cold water; *Thin paste* is made by blending 1 part cornflour with 2 parts water.

Thick paste is really like a batter – it is used to coat the ingredients, leaving no liquid in the dish. Thin paste is a glazing paste, which is added to the gravy left in the wok after the food is removed; this is then heated and made smooth, and poured over the food as a sauce.

Blending of Flavours and Seasonings

A dish is usually made up of more than one ingredient – in the few exceptions when only a single item is used, a number of different seasonings are always blended in to give the dish a harmonious balance and contrast.

The materials used in a dish are divided between the 'main' ingredient, and 'supplementary' ingredient(s). The main ingredient is the major item (usually meat, poultry or fish), and the supplementary ingredients (usually vegetables) are used to give the dish a contrast in colour, flavour and texture.

In selecting the ingredients for a dish or a course of dishes, attention should be paid to:

1. *Quantity:* the main ingredient's colour, aroma, flavour and texture should be paramount. If there is no marked distinction between the main and supplementary ingredients, then equal proportions should be used.

2. *Flavour:* the main ingredient's flavour should dominate the dish; the supplementary ingredients should be lighter in flavour. If the main ingredient itself is light in flavour (such as bean-curd or *tofu,* etc.), then heavily seasoned supplementary ingredients should complement the main one.
3. *Texture:* the texture of the various ingredients can be similar, or in contrast which offers a more interesting result.
4. *Colour:* colour will affect presentation of the dish and its flavour – overcooked ingredients lose their bright colours as well as their natural flavours.

There are five basic flavours in Chinese cooking:
1. **Sweet** (flavouring agents: sugar, honey, fruit, jam, etc).
2. **Sour** (vinegar, plum sauce, tomato sauce, etc).
3. **Bitter** (almond, orange peel, herbs, etc).
4. **Hot** (chilli, chilli sauce, peppers, ginger, mustard, etc).
5. **Salty** (salt, soy sauce, soybean paste, etc).

Two additional flavours are often included in most regional styles of cooking:
6. **Fragrant or aromatic xiang** (wine, garlic, spring onions, Sichuan pepper, sesame seeds, sesame oil, spices, etc).
7. **Delicious xian** (monosodium glutamate, oyster sauce, shrimp sauce, chicken and meat stock, etc). It is interesting to note here that the Chinese character for *xian* is made up by joining 'fish' with 'goat' – the Chinese seem to have discovered long ago that the combination of fish and meat produces a perfect balance of flavours. In a different context, *xian* also means 'fresh', therefore, it would seem that the Chinese also link freshness with deliciousness.

Out of these basic flavours, a Chinese cook can create several combination flavours – such as sweet and sour, hot and sour, aromatic and hot, etc.

The question of using monosodium glutamate (MSG) in Chinese cooking has been controversial in some circles. I think that you should know a few facts about it before making up your own mind on this matter.

First of all, *monosodium glutamate* (MSG) is the sodium salt of glutamic acid, an amino acid and one of the most abundant and important components of proteins. Glutamic acid and its various salts like potassium, calcium and so on are generically referred to as 'glutamate', which is a natural component found in virtually all foods such as meat, fish, milk, and vegetables.

The Chinese have been using MSG in its liquid form as soy sauce for centuries, but the chemical compound known as monosodium glutamate was first discovered by a German named Ritthauson in 1866, and its use as a flavouring agent in cooking wasn't utilized until 1908, when the professor of chemistry at the Imperial University of Tokyo, Ikeda Kikue, extracted MSG from seaweed, which became *Aji-No-Moto* ('the element of taste' in Japanese).

Then in 1923, the Chinese started making their own MSG from wheat protein, known as *Ve-Tsin* ('the essence of taste'), or Gourmet Powder. Its popularity was phenomenal – within years it truly became an indispensable item to both the catering trade and the better-off households – for as the makers claim on the package: 'A sprinkling of Ve-Tsin will bring out the full natural flavour of your dishes and render them surprisingly delicious.'

Extensive research conducted worldwide clearly demonstrates that MSG is safe for human consumption, since it contains less sodium than the common table salt we use everyday. Some Chinese restaurants may claim that they do not use any MSG in their dishes, but what about soy sauce, oyster sauce and all the other bean sauces? All these condiments contain MSG – that's why they taste so *xian* (delicious).

Should you decide to use MSG at home, just remember that you only need a tiny amount of the powder each time. Do not use it in every single dish you are serving. Another point to bear in mind is that it should never be added to the food until toward the end of cooking – nor should it be sprinkled on at the table like salt and pepper – for in order to acquire its proper effect, it has to be dissolved completely with the food at the last stage of cooking.

The Principles of Seasoning

Marinating the raw ingredient with basic seasonings (salt, pepper, sugar, soy sauce, vinegar, wine, oil, cornflour, etc) creates a basic flavour for the dish, or diffuses certain strong flavour in the ingredient.

Seasonings added to the ingredients during cooking enhance the flavour of the food.

After cooking, supplementary seasoning added to the dish in the form of garnishes (sesame oil, spring onions, coriander, etc) further enhances the appearance and flavour of the dish. Also in certain cooking methods, such as deep-frying, steaming, rapid-boiling (poaching) or blanching, etc, seasonings cannot be added during cooking, therefore seasonings in the form of dips or garnishes can make up for any flavour deficiency.

Other points to remember are:

Balance: you should take note of what is the correct flavour of the dish. If it calls for several different spices or seasonings, make the leading flavour stand out.

The nature of the ingredient: fresh foods should not be seasoned too highly, or their original delicacy will be lost. Food that has a strong flavour can be highly seasoned in order to reduce or eliminate the strong flavour.

The climate: people's taste changes with the seasons – generally they like light food during hot seasons; and heavier, rich food in colder and milder seasons.

You will find the details of all the 'flavouring agents' plus other special ingredients in the Glossary at the end of this book. But before you start doing any serious Chinese cooking, you should just consider the following two items:

Cooking Oil

The most commonly used oil in Chinese restaurants is a blended vegetable oil that is sold in a 20 litre drum. This is not practical for the home, so I recommend a cooking oil made from peanuts (groundnuts), soya beans, rape seeds or sunflower seeds. Corn oil and olive oil are not really suitable for Chinese food, and sesame seed oil is meant for garnishing only, therefore it should never be used for cooking.

Whichever type of vegetable oil you choose (my personal favourites are sunflower and soy oils), it should be seasoned before use – the Chinese term is *lian* (refine; temper with fire). The idea is to neutralize the flavour of a particular oil, so that it does not dominate the flavour of the dish.

How to Season Raw Vegetable Oil

Pour 600ml (about 1 pint) vegetable oil into a pre-heated wok or saucepan over a high heat, add 2–3 small pieces of peeled ginger root. In a few minutes, the ginger pieces should rise to the surface. Now watch the colour of the ginger: when it turns from pale yellow to dark brown, turn off the heat and let the oil cool down a little before removing the ginger pieces. Then store the seasoned oil in a container.

The seasoned oil can be reused a number of times. This is one of the reasons why simple vegetable dishes taste so good – because they have been cooked in oil in which meat, poultry, etc has been cooked. It may be necessary to filter and season the oil again. After a while, the oil may become rancid, then it should be discarded. In a restaurant kitchen, certain dishes require freshly seasoned oil, and this will be indicated in the recipes.

Basic Stock

This is the very first item a Chinese cook prepares when starting work in the kitchen each day. It is used not only as the basis for soups, but also for general use in cooking instead of water whenever liquid is required. Refrigerated when cool, it will keep up to 4–5 days; alternatively it can be frozen in small containers and defrosted as required.

1.25kg ($2^1/_2$–$2^3/_4$lb) chicken pieces (excluding breastmeat)
1.25kg ($2^1/_2$–$2^3/_4$lb) pork spare-ribs
7 litres (12 pints) water*
3–4 large pieces ginger root, unpeeled and crushed
3–4 spring onions, each tied into a knot (see fig. 17)
3–4 tablespoons Chinese rice wine (or dry sherry)

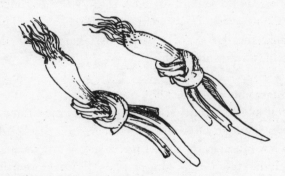

Fig. 17. Spring onions tied into knots.

1. Trim off and discard excess fat from the chicken and pork. Place the chicken and pork in a large pot with the cold water, ginger and spring onions. Bring to the boil and skim off the scum.
2. Reduce the heat but keep it on the boil, uncovered, for at least 2–3 hours; by then the liquid should be reduced by about one-third.
3. Strain the stock, discarding the chicken and pork pieces, ginger and spring onions; add the wine and return to the boil, simmer for 2–3 minutes. Now it is ready for use.

* If you do not possess a large enough pot to hold 12 pints of water, by all means reduce all the ingredients proportionately.

NB Since all restaurants have duck dishes on the menu, the carcass and other bits and pieces of the duck are often added to the stock, which makes it that much more delicious. This is known as **Superior stock**.

3
COLD STARTERS
(APPETIZERS)

'White-Cut' Pork, page 49
'White-Cut' Chicken, page 50
Poached Prawns with Special Sauce, page 52
Five-Spice Beef, page 53
Soy-Braised Duck, page 54
Bang-Bang Chicken, page 56
Jellyfish with Mustard Dressing, page 58
Pickled Cucumber, page 59

See also:
Crispy 'Seaweed', page 74
'Smoked' Fish, page 84
Char Siu – Honey Roasted Pork, page 100
Roast Duck – Cantonese Style, page 102

One of the advantages of these dishes is that all of them can be prepared and cooked well in advance – hours or even a couple of days before – since they are to be served cold. Another point to bear in mind is that if any of these dishes is made in fairly large quantity, you need not serve all of it, but save some for another day – unless you are catering for a big party. Of course, all these dishes are ideal for buffet-style meals or party food.

Very little cooking skill is required for any of these dishes, so there is no reason why you should not attain a 'Restaurant Quality' rating of 95%–100%.

'WHITE-CUT' PORK 白切肉

Serves 18–20 as a starter, or 10–12 as a main course.

Preparation & cooking time: 1 hour & cooling time.

'White-cut' is a Chinese cooking method used for white meats that are very fresh and tender. They are cooked in large pieces in a relatively short time, then the heat is turned off and the remainder of the cooking is carried out by the retaining heat.

Besides being served cold either on its own or as a part of an assorted hors d'oeuvre, any leftovers can be used for a number of recipes which call for ready-cooked meat, such as Twice-Cooked Pork (see page 145).

1 kg (2¹/₄ lb) leg of tender pork, boned but not skinned

For the sauce:
1–2 teaspoons finely chopped garlic
1 tablespoon finely chopped spring onions
1 teaspoon caster sugar
4 tablespoons light soy sauce
1 teaspoon sesame oil
1 teaspoon red chilli oil (optional)

Place the pork, tied together in one piece, in a large pot, add cold water to cover, and bring it to a rolling boil. Skim off the scum and simmer gently under cover for about 1 hour. Leave the pork in the liquid to cool, under cover, for at least 2–3 hours before removing it to cool with the skin side up for a further 4–6 hours.

To serve: cut off the skin, leaving a very thin layer of fat on top like a ham joint. Cut the meat into small thin slices across the grain, arrange neatly on a plate; mix the sauce ingredients, and pour the sauce evenly all over the pork.

'WHITE-CUT' CHICKEN
白切鷄

Serves 8–12 as a starter, or 4 as a main course.

Preparation & cooking time: 25 mins & cooling time.

1 whole chicken (about 1.25kg (2¹/₂–2³/₄lb) without giblets)
about 1.5 litres (2¹/₂ pints) water
2–3 spring onions, each tied into a knot (see page 45)
2–3 pieces ginger root, unpeeled and crushed
3–4 tablespoons Chinese rice wine
1 tablespoon salt

For the sauce:
6–8 tablespoons light soy sauce
1 tablespoon caster sugar
2 tablespoons finely chopped spring onions
1 teaspoon finely chopped garlic (optional)
1 teaspoon chilli sauce (optional)
2 teaspoons sesame oil

Clean the chicken well, then pat dry thoroughly with kitchen paper. Bring the water to a rolling boil in a saucepan or pot, gently lower the chicken into the water with its breast-side up, and add the spring onion knots, ginger and rice wine. Cover the pan with a tight-fitting lid and bring the water back to the boil, then add the salt and reduce the heat and simmer for 15–20 minutes only, keeping the lid very tightly shut all the time. Then remove the pan from the heat and leave to cool for 6–8 hours; the bird will continue to cook gently in the hot water provided you put something heavy on top of the lid to make sure there is no escape of heat.

About an hour before you serve it, remove the chicken and drain. (The liquid can be used as a base for stock making.) Chop the chicken into 22–24 bite-size pieces with a Chinese cleaver (see pages 38–39), then reassemble the bird on a serving platter. If you do not possess a cleaver, then carve the meat off the bone, and arrange neatly on a serving dish.

Mix all the sauce ingredients with a little liquid in which the chicken has been cooked. Either pour it evenly all over the chicken, or put it out on 2–3 small saucers to be used as a dip.

POACHED PRAWNS WITH SPECIAL SAUCE
熗明蝦

Serves 4–6.

Preparation & cooking time: 10–15 mins

250g (8oz) uncooked and unshelled prawns, headless
pinch of salt

For the sauce:
2 spring onions, thinly shredded
about 1 tablespoon thinly shredded fresh ginger
1–2 fresh green or red chillies, seeded and thinly shredded*
1 tablespoon vegetable oil
2 tablespoons light soy sauce
1 tablespoon rice vinegar
a few drops of sesame oil

Clean the prawns well. Poach them in a pan of salted boiling water for 1 minute only, then turn off the heat and leave the prawns in the hot water for another minute or two. Remove and drain, then place on a serving plate.

Place the spring onions, ginger and chillies in a small heat-proof bowl. Heat the oil until hot and pour it over them. Add the soy sauce, vinegar and sesame oil, stir to blend well.

To serve, each person picks up a prawn with fingers, peels off the shell, leaving the tail piece on as a handle, and dips the prawn into the sauce before eating.

***NB** Handle fresh hot chillies with extra care. Avoid touching other parts of your body with your hands after handling chillies, and always wash your hands well immediately afterwards as the irritant in them will cause a burning sensation on contact with your skin.

FIVE-SPICE BEEF 五香鹵牛肉

Serves 10–12 as a starter, or 4–6 as a main course.

Preparation & cooking time: 55–60 mins & cooling time.

The liquid in which the beef has been cooked should be reserved for cooking other meat or poultry, and is known as Lu Zhi 'Master Gravy'.

750g (1¹/₂lb) shin of beef
2–3 spring onions, each tied into a knot (see page 45)
3–4 pieces of ginger root, unpeeled
3–4 tablespoons Chinese spirit or brandy
about 1.5 litres (2¹/₂ pints) basic stock (see page 45)
1 teaspoon salt
4 tablespoons light soy sauce
3 tablespoons dark soy sauce
1 tablespoon five-spice powder
125g (4oz) rock candy or crystal sugar

To garnish:
1 tablespoon finely chopped spring onions
1 teaspoon sesame oil

Cut the beef into 2–3 long strips, place them with the spring onions, ginger, brandy and stock in a pot, bring to the boil and skim off the scum; simmer gently under cover for 20–25 minutes.

Add the salt, soy sauces, spice and sugar, return to the boil, then simmer, covered, for 25–30 minutes longer.

Remove the beef to cool. Just before serving, slice it thinly across the grain, arrange neatly on a plate, and garnish with finely chopped spring onions and sesame oil. Filter the 'gravy' and refrigerate when cold. It can be used again and again. The more you use it, the better it is.

SOY-BRAISED DUCK
醬鴨

Serves 10–12 as a starter, or 4–6 as a main course.

Preparation & cooking time: about 1 hour & cooling time.

Chicken or any other type of meat can be cooked in the same way. Also if you do not want to cook a whole duck or chicken, by all means use jointed pieces – halves, quarters or just legs, wings, etc, of the bird can be used.

One 2kg (4¹/₂lb) duckling (with or without giblets)
2 teaspoons salt
about 1.2 litres (2 pints) 'Master Gravy' (see page 53)
about 600ml (1 pint) stock or water
3–4 spring onions, each tied into a knot (see page 45)
3–4 pieces of fresh ginger root, unpeeled
5–6 star anise pieces
2–3 cinnamon sticks   } or 1 tablespoon five-spice powder
1 tablespoon Sichuan red peppercorns
4–5 tablespoons Shao Hsing rice wine or brandy
2–3 tablespoons light soy sauce
125g (4oz) rock candy or crystal sugar

Clean the duck well, then blanch it in a pot of boiling water. Remove and rinse in cold water; pat dry with kitchen paper and rub the cavity with the salt.

Bring the 'Master Gravy' with stock or water to the boil, add the duck (with giblets, if using) with the spring onion knots, ginger, spices, wine, soy sauce and sugar; bring to the boil, then simmer gently under cover for 45–50 minutes. Leave the duck to cool in the liquid for 2–3 hours or longer.

To serve: remove the duck and drain. Chop the meat into small bite-sized pieces (see pages 38–39), arrange neatly on a platter and serve either on its own, or as part of an assorted hors d'oeuvres.

Strain the gravy, and pour about 2–3 tablespoons over the duck. Refrigerate the rest when cool for future use.

BANG-BANG CHICKEN
棒棒鷄

Serves 8–10.

Preparation & cooking time: 45 mins & cooling time.

This very popular Sichuan dish is also known as Bon-Bon Chicken in some restaurants, so called because the meat is tenderised by being banged with a stick (*bon* in Chinese).

about 1 litre (2 pints) water
1 whole chicken (about 1kg (2^1/$_4$lb) without giblets)
2–3 spring onions, each tied into a knot (see page 45)
2–3 pieces ginger root, unpeeled and crushed
1 teaspoon salt
1 tablespoon sesame oil
shredded lettuce leaves, to garnish

For the sauce:
2 tablespoons light soy sauce
1 teaspoon caster sugar
2 tablespoons finely chopped spring onions
1 teaspoon red chilli oil
^{1}/$_2$ teaspoon ground Sichuan red peppercorn
1 teaspoon white sesame seeds
2 tablespoons sesame paste or peanut butter creamed with a little
    sesame oil

Bring the water to the boil, add the chicken with the spring onion knots and the ginger, bring back to the boil, then add the salt and reduce the heat and simmer for 30–35 minutes, keeping the lid very tightly shut all the time. Then turn off the heat and leave to cool for 3–4 hours under cover.

Remove the chicken, drain and pat dry with kitchen paper. Brush on a coating of sesame oil, and leave to dry for another 10–15 minutes before carving the meat off the bones, pound with a rolling pin to loosen the meat, then tear all the meat into shreds with your fingers. Place on top of the lettuce leaves.

Mix about 150ml (5fl oz) of the liquid in which the chicken was cooked with all the sauce ingredients and pour over the chicken. Mix and toss at the table just before serving.

JELLYFISH WITH MUSTARD DRESSING
凉拌海蜇

Serves 4–6.

Preparation & cooking time: 20–25 mins & soaking time.

Dried jellyfish comes in 500g (1lb) slabs; the surplus from this recipe will keep in the refrigerator for several weeks.

125g (4oz) dried jellyfish
about 10cm (4") cucumber

For the dressing:
1 teaspoon salt
1 tablespoon caster sugar
2–3 tablespoons white rice vinegar
1 tablespoon English mustard powder
1 teaspoon sesame oil

Soak the dried jellyfish in warm water for about 3 hours; wash thoroughly in fresh water and drain. Thinly shred into about 6cm (2½") long strips. Blanch in boiling water for a few minutes, rinse in cold water and drain, place on a plate.

Cut the cucumber into about 5cm (2") long shreds, mix with the jellyfish. Mix the dressing and pour it evenly all over the dish. Mix well just before serving.

PICKLED CUCUMBER
凉拌青瓜

Serves 6–8.

Preparation time: about 10–15 mins & marinating time.

1 medium-sized cucumber
1 teaspoon salt
1 tablespoon sugar
1 tablespoon red rice vinegar
$^1/_3$ teaspoon red chilli oil (optional)
a few drops of sesame oil

Split the cucumber, unpeeled, in half lengthwise, scrape off and discard the seeds, then cut across into thick chunks. Sprinkle with the salt and mix thoroughly. Marinate for at least 10 minutes – longer if possible – then pour the juice away. Mix with the sugar, vinegar and red chilli oil (if using). Garnish with sesame oil just before serving.

4

SOUPS

Have you ever wondered how the Chinese can make such delicious soups out of what appear to be very simple materials? The secret is, of course, the stock that is used as a basis for the soup (see page 45), and the addition of MSG in the seasonings (see page 42). A Chinese cook can make a soup fit for the gods merely by adding a handful of fresh greens to boiling water and pouring the whole mixture over a pinch of MSG and salt in a serving bowl.

The ingredients for the soup, either raw or part-cooked, and almost always cut into small, thin shreds or slices, are rapidly poached in the boiling stock for less than a minute, so that they retain their delicate texture and flavour.

Do not use a stock cube as a short cut, since the commercially manufactured produce contains quite different constituents; it has an entirely un-Chinese taste.

Allow about 175ml (6 fl oz) stock per person when making soup; therefore 600ml (1 pint) will serve four with the addition of other solid ingredients.

Like the Cold Starters, very little cooking skill is required for making any of these soups, therefore you should have no difficulty in achieving a 98%–100% success rate, provided you have a good stock to start with, and the right seasonings.

FISH BALLS AND WATERCRESS SOUP
魚丸洋菜湯

Serves 4.

Preparation & cooking time: 10 mins approx.

1 small packet (200g) ready-made fish balls
1 bunch watercress
600ml (1 pint) stock (see page 45)
salt and pepper to taste
a dash of MSG (optional)
finely chopped spring onions to garnish

Cut each fish ball in half; trim and wash the watercress.

Bring the stock to a rolling boil and add the fish balls, return to the boil and cook for 1 minute, adjust the seasonings before adding the watercress. Serve at once with the garnish.

HOT AND SOUR SOUP
酸辣湯

Serves 4–6.

Preparation & cooking time: 10–15 mins

Hot chillies should never be added to this soup – the hotness comes from liberal use of ground white pepper.

3–4 dried Chinese mushrooms, soaked (see Glossary)
100g (4oz) pork or chicken (raw or pre-cooked)
50g (2oz) sliced bamboo shoots, drained
1 cake bean-curd (tofu)
900ml (1¹/₂ pints) stock (see page 45)
1 tablespoon Shao Hsing rice wine
1 tablespoon light soy sauce
1 tablespoon red or white rice vinegar
1 teaspoon ground white pepper
1 egg, lightly beaten
1 tablespoon thick cornflour paste (see page 40)
1 teaspoon salt
¹/₃ teaspoon MSG (optional)

Squeeze dry the soaked mushrooms and discard any hard stalks. Thinly shred the mushrooms, meat, bamboo shoots and bean-curd.

Bring the stock to a rolling boil, stir in the mushrooms, meat, bamboo shoots and bean-curd, bring back to the boil, now add the wine, soy sauce, vinegar and pepper, bring back to the boil once more, then pour the beaten egg very slowly into the soup, stirring at the same time. Finally, stir in gently the cornflour paste to thicken the soup, before pouring it into a soup tureen with the salt and MSG, if using, at the bottom; blend well and serve hot!

SWEETCORN AND CRABMEAT/ CHICKEN SOUP
蟹肉／鷄肉粟米湯

Serves 4.

Preparation & cooking time: 10–15 mins

100g (4oz) crabmeat, thawed if frozen or
    175g (6oz) chicken breast meat, coarsely chopped
$^1/_2$ teaspoon finely chopped fresh ginger root
2 egg whites
2–3 tablespoons milk
1 tablespoon thick cornflour paste (see page 40)
600ml (1 pint) stock (see page 45)
225g (8oz) can creamed sweetcorn (American style)
salt and pepper to taste
a dash of MSG (optional)
finely chopped spring onions to garnish

Flake the crabmeat (or chop the chicken meat), then mix with the ginger. Beat the egg whites until frothy, then add the milk and cornflour paste, and beat again until smooth. Blend in the crabmeat or chicken meat.

Bring the stock to the boil, add the creamed sweetcorn and bring back to the boil. Stir in the crabmeat or chicken and egg white mixture, adjust the seasonings and stir gently until well blended. As soon as the soup thickens, garnish with the spring onions and serve.

CHICKEN AND MUSHROOM SOUP
鷄片蔴菇湯

Serves 4.

Preparation & cooking time: 15 mins approx.

100-150g (4–5oz) chicken breast meat
100g (4oz) white mushrooms
2–3 egg whites, beaten
1 tablespoon thick cornflour paste (see page 40)
600ml (1 pint) stock (see page 45)
salt to taste
a dash of MSG (optional)
a few drops of sesame oil (optional)
fresh coriander leaves to garnish

Cut the chicken meat into thin slices about the size of postage stamps. Thinly slice the mushrooms. Blend the egg whites with the cornflour paste, making the mixture smooth.

Bring the stock to a rolling boil, stir in the chicken first followed by the mushrooms, return to the boil, then very slowly pour in the egg white and cornflour mixture, stirring constantly. As soon as the soup thickens, add salt, MSG, if using, and sesame oil, and serve immediately with the garnish.

WEST LAKE BEEF SOUP
西湖牛肉湯

Serves 4.

Preparation & cooking time: 10–15 mins

100g (4oz) beef steak
2 teaspoons light soy sauce
¹/₂ teaspoon soft brown sugar
1 tablespoon Shao Hsing rice wine
2 tablespoons thick cornflour paste (see page 40)
a few drops of sesame oil
600ml (1 pint) stock (see page 45)
1 whole egg, lightly beaten
100g (4oz) shelled peas
salt and pepper to taste
dash of MSG (optional)
finely chopped spring onions to garnish

Coarsely chop the steak, marinate in the soy sauce, sugar, wine, about 1 teaspoon cornflour paste and sesame oil for 5–6 minutes.

Bring the stock to the boil, slowly pour in the beaten egg, stirring constantly. Add the peas and bring back to the boil, then add the steak, and stir to separate the bits. Thicken the soup with the remaining cornflour paste. Adjust the seasonings and serve with the garnish.

MIXED VEGETABLES SOUP
什錦素菜湯

Serves 4.

Preparation & cooking time: 15–20 mins approx.

Almost any type of vegetable can be used in this soup – choose two, three or four different items from the following list.

50–85g (2–3oz) each of black/white mushrooms, bamboo shoots, carrot, asparagus, baby corn cobs, spinach, lettuce, cucumber, Chinese leaves, or tomato, etc
1 cake bean-curd (tofu)
600ml (1 pint) stock (see page 45)
1 tablespoon light soy sauce
salt and pepper to taste
dash of MSG (optional)
a few drops of sesame oil (optional)
finely chopped spring onions to garnish

Cut your selection of vegetables and the bean-curd into roughly uniform shape and size (i.e. shreds, slices, cubes, etc). Bring the stock to the boil and add the vegetables, bearing in mind that certain ingredients require a longer cooking time than others, so cook these first, then add the others after an appropriate interval.

Do not overcook this, otherwise the vegetables will go soggy and lose their crispness as well as their delicate flavour. As a rule of thumb, boil carrot and baby corn cobs (if raw) for 2–3 minutes; mushrooms, bean-curd, asparagus, Chinese leaves, etc, for about 2 minutes; spinach, lettuce and watercress for less than 1 minute.

Adjust the seasonings (including the sesame oil) to taste and serve hot with the garnish.

DUCK SOUP
鴨骨湯

Serves 6–8.

Preparation & cooking time: about 35–40 mins

This dish is traditionally served at the end of a duck dinner, as it is made from the carcass of the Peking Duck (see page 104).

1 duck carcass (plus giblets if available)
2–3 small slices ginger root
6–8 small dried Chinese mushrooms, soaked (see Glossary)
450g (1lb) Chinese leaves
1–2 spring onions, finely chopped
salt and pepper to taste

Break up the carcass, place it together with the giblets and any other bits and pieces in a large pot or pan, cover with about 1.5 litres (2½ pints) water, add the ginger root and bring to the boil. Skim off the impurities floating on the surface, and simmer gently for at least 30 minutes.

Squeeze dry the soaked mushrooms and discard any hard stalks. Thinly slice the Chinese leaves, add them and the mushrooms to the soup, continue cooking for 10–15 minutes, add the spring onions, and adjust the seasonings. Serve hot.

NB When serving, do warn your guests that there might be small bits of bones in the soup.

5

DEEP-FRIED DISHES

There are different variations of deep-frying (ZHA) in Chinese cooking:

(a) *Neat Deep-frying:* the raw ingredients are not coated with batter or flour – e.g. Crispy 'Seaweed'.

(b) *Dry Deep-frying:* the raw ingredients are coated with dry flour or breadcrumbs – e.g. 'Butterfly' Prawns.

(c) *Soft Deep-frying:* the raw ingredients are coated with batter – e.g. Lemon Chicken.

(d) *Crisp Deep-frying:* the ingredients are boiled or steamed first, then deep-fried for crispness – e.g. Deep-fried Squid.

You will find the conical-shaped wok is an ideal utensil for deep-frying as it requires far less oil than a flat-bottomed deep-fryer, and it has more depth (which means more heat) and more frying surface (which means more food can be cooked more quickly at one go). Furthermore, since the wok has a larger capacity at the top than at the base, when the oil level rises as the ingredients are added there is little chance of the oil over-flowing and causing the pan to catch fire as often happens with a conventional deep-fryer.

Heat and timing are the two vital points to watch here. Once you can master these, then the success rate should be no less than 90–100%.

PRAWN CRACKERS
蝦片

Serves 4–6.

Cooking time: 5 mins

Ready-made prawn crackers in packets are widely available in supermarkets throughout the country (see also Shopping Guide). Ideal as an accompaniment to drinks or cocktails, they can also be served with Chinese meals for any occasion, hot or cold.

oil for deep-frying
25g (1oz) prawn crackers

Heat the oil in a wok or deep-fryer to hot (about 180°C/350°F), then turn the heat down to moderate (160°C/325°F) and fry 6–8 prawn crackers at a time. They puff-up rather dramatically in a matter of seconds, and when they are expanded fully, they become snow-white in colour and about four times larger in size. Now remove them immediately with a strainer or sieve, shake off excess oil and drain on kitchen paper.

After you have cooked the first two batches, heat the oil again to the required temperature. If the cooked crackers are not to be served within the next hour or two, they should be stored in an airtight container in order to retain their crispness; or they can be re-crispened by heating in a low oven for 5–6 minutes.

CRISPY 'SEAWEED'
乾貝鬆

Serves 6–8 as a starter.

Preparation & cooking time: 15–20 mins & drying time.

You will be pleasantly surprised to learn that this exotic and very popular dish available in Chinese restaurants is in fact nothing more than fried green cabbage! It is not too difficult to prepare and cook at home; the secret is to make sure the leaves are completely dry before frying.

Some restaurants garnish this dish with dried scallops, which are prohibitively expensive and extremely tedious to prepare, so many others opt for the easy substitute of ready-made ground fried fish or roasted almonds.

450g (1lb) spring greens
oil for deep-frying
1 teaspoon caster sugar
$^1/_2$ teaspoon salt
pinch of MSG (optional)

To garnish (optional):
1 tablespoon ground fried fish (see Glossary), or
    1 tablespoon roasted, flaked and crushed almonds

Separate the dark outer leaves (reserve the pale-coloured hearts for other use) and clean well with a damp cloth – do not wash in water as they will take too long to dry. Cut off the hard stalks in the centre of each leaf (see fig. 18a).

Pile the leaves on top of each other and roll into a tight 'sausage', then thinly cut into fine shreds (see fig. 18b). Spread the shreds out to dry for at least 30 minutes or 2–3 hours.

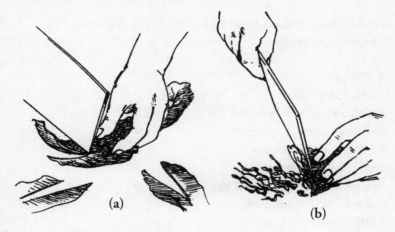

(a)　(b)

Fig. 18. Cutting and shredding the spring greens.

To cook: heat the oil in a wok or deep-fryer until hot (180°C/350°F). Deep-fry the shredded greens in batches; stir to separate them. Remove as soon as they are crispy, *but before the colour starts to change from dark green to light brown,* with a strainer or sieve. Drain and sprinkle the seasonings evenly all over. Serve with or without garnish.

The 'seaweed' will stay crisp for several hours; or it can be re-crispened for a few minutes in a medium-hot oven if gone limp.

NB The colour of the oil turns green after cooking the 'seaweed', so it should not be re-used for cooking anything other than green vegetables (such as spinach, broccoli or green cabbage, etc).

CRISPY WANTONS WITH SWEET AND SOUR SAUCE

甜酸炸雲吞

Serves 4–6 as a starter.

Preparation & cooking time: 25–30 mins.

18–24 ready-made Wanton skins (from Oriental stores)
oil for deep-frying

For the sauce:
1 tablespoon oil
2 tablespoons soft brown sugar
3 tablespoons rice vinegar
1 tablespoon light soy sauce
1 tablespoon tomato sauce
3–4 tablespoons stock (see page 45) or water
pinch of MSG (optional)
1 tablespoon thick cornflour paste (see page 40)

Pinch the centre of each Wanton skin and twist around to form a floral shape.

Fig. 19. Forming a floral shape.

Deep-fry the Wantons in moderately hot oil (160°C/325°F) for 1–2 minutes, or until crispy. Remove and drain.

To make the sauce: heat the oil in a wok or saucepan, add the sugar, vinegar, soy sauce, tomato sauce and stock or water; stir to blend well and bring to boil. Now add the MSG (if using) and thicken the sauce with the cornflour paste, making it smooth, and serve with the crispy Wanton skins.

SESAME PRAWN TOASTS
芝麻蝦

Serves 6–8 as a starter.

Preparation & cooking time: 40–45 mins.

For best results, use uncooked prawns for this dish, as the ready-cooked prawns will not have the same texture or flavour.

225g (8oz) uncooked, shelled prawns
25g (1oz) lard or shortening
salt and pepper to taste
1 tablespoon egg white
1 teaspoon finely chopped spring onions
$^{1}/_{2}$ teaspoon finely chopped fresh ginger root
1 tablespoon Chinese rice wine (optional)
1 tablespoon thick cornflour paste (see page 40)
about 115–140g (4–5oz) white sesame seeds
6 large slices white bread
oil for deep-frying
Crispy 'Seaweed' or shredded lettuce leaves to garnish (optional)

Mince the prawns and lard until they form a smooth paste. Mix with the salt, pepper, egg white, spring onions, ginger, wine and cornflour paste.

Spread the sesame seeds evenly on a large plate or tray. Spread the prawn paste thickly on one side of each slice of bread, then place, spread-side down, on the surface of the sesame seeds.

Heat the oil in a wok or deep-fryer until medium hot (180°C/350°F), deep-fry the 'toasts', spread-side down, 2–3 slices at a time, for about 2–3 minutes or until they start to turn golden. Remove and drain.

To serve: trim off the dark brown crusts, cut each slice into 6–8 fingers. Serve on a bed of Crispy 'Seaweed' or shredded lettuce leaves.

'BUTTERFLY' PRAWNS
炸鳳尾蝦

Serves 18–20 as a starter, or 8–10 as a main course.

Preparation & cooking time: 35–40 mins & marinating time.

These headless prawns are about 8–10cm (3–4") long and sold in their shells, you should get 18–20 prawns per 450g (1lb).

450g (1lb) uncooked giant or king prawns, headless
salt and pepper to taste
1 tablespoon light soy sauce
1 tablespoon Chinese rice wine
2 teaspoons cornflour
2 eggs, beaten
4–5 tablespoons breadcrumbs
oil for deep-frying
coriander leaves to garnish (optional)

Shell the prawns but leave the tails on (see fig. 20a). Split each prawn in half, leaving the tails still firmly attached.

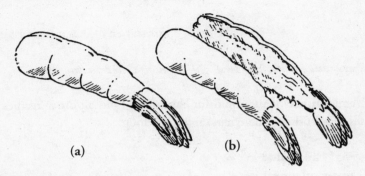

(a)　　　　　　　　　　(b)

Fig. 20. Preparing the prawns.

Marinate the prawns in the salt, pepper, soy sauce, wine and cornflour for 10–15 minutes.

To cook: pick up half of a prawn by the tail, dip it in the egg, then roll it in the breadcrumbs before lowering it into hot (190°C/375°F) oil. Deep-fry in batches until golden brown. Remove with a strainer or sieve and drain.

Serve garnished with coriander leaves, or on a bed of Crispy 'Seaweed' (see page 74) ungarnished.

DEEP-FRIED SQUID
椒鹽鮮魷

Serves 6–8 as a starter, or 4 as a main course.

Preparation & cooking time: 30–40 mins & marinating time.

The ideal size of the squid for this recipe (and all other recipes in this book) should be 15cm (about 6") long.

450g (1lb) squid
1 teaspoon ginger juice*
1 tablespoon Chinese rice wine
about 575ml (1 pint) boiling water
oil for deep-frying
coriander leaves to garnish
spicy salt and pepper** to serve

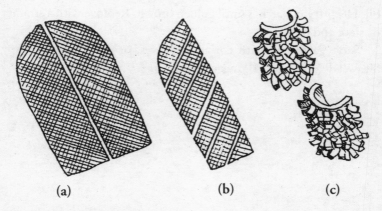

(a)   (b)   (c)

Fig. 21. Preparing the squid.

Clean the squid by discarding the head and the transparent backbone as well as the ink bag; peel off the thin skin, then wash and dry well (often this part will already have been done by the fishmonger).

Open up the squid and score the *inside* of the flesh in a criss-cross pattern (see fig. 21a). Cut into pieces about the size of a large postage stamp (see fig. 21b), then marinate with ginger juice and wine for 25–30 minutes.

Blanch in a pan of boiling water for 25–30 seconds – each piece will curl up and the criss-cross pattern will open out to resemble ears of corn (see fig. 21c). Remove and drain. Dry well.

Deep-fry in hot oil (190°C/375°F) for 15–20 seconds only, remove quickly and drain. Garnish with coriander leaves and serve with spicy salt and pepper.

*Ginger Juice Mix finely chopped or grated fresh ginger root with an equal quantity of cold water and place in damp muslin, then twist tightly to extract the juice. Alternatively, crush the ginger in a garlic press.

**Spicy Salt and Pepper Mix 1 tablespoon salt with 2 teaspoons ground Sichuan peppercorns and 1 teaspoon five-spice powder (see Glossary), heat them in a dry pan for about 2–3 minutes over a low heat, stirring constantly. This quantity is sufficient for at least six servings.

'SMOKED' FISH
燻魚

Serves 8–10 as a starter, or 4 as a main course.

Preparation & cooking time: about 1 hour & cooling time.

The interesting point about this dish is that the fish is not actually smoked. It acquires a smoky flavour from being first marinated and braised in a spicy sauce, then deep-fried in hot oil and marinated in the sauce once more before serving.

450g (1lb) firm white fish fillets (cod, haddock or coley)
about 280ml (¹/₂ pint) stock (see page 45)
oil for deep-frying

For the marinade:
2 tablespoons light soy sauce
1 tablespoon dark soy sauce
3 tablespoons Chinese rice wine
2–3 tablespoons soft brown sugar
2 teaspoons five-spice powder
2 spring onions, finely chopped
1 tablespoon finely chopped fresh ginger root

Pat dry the fish with kitchen paper or towels, and keep the skin on. Marinate in the marinade for at least 30 minutes, then add the stock and bring to the boil; simmer for 10 minutes, then remove the fish and drain. Reserve the sauce.

Deep-fry the fish in very hot oil (190°C/375°F) for 4–5 minutes or until golden and crisp, remove and immerse in the sauce. Leave to cool for 2–3 hours before taking the fish out to dry.

Strain the sauce and store in the refrigerator for up to 4–5 days to be used again.

Cut the fish into small slices and serve cold.

LEMON CHICKEN
檸檬鷄

Serves 4.

Preparation & cooking time: 20–25 mins & marinating time.

Lemon Sauce is a Cantonese specialty – it has a delicate piquant flavour that rivals favourably the ubiquitous sweet and sour sauce served in most Chinese restaurants.

450g (1lb) chicken breast fillets
salt and pepper to taste
1 tablespoon Chinese rice wine
1 egg, beaten
2 tablespoons plain flour blended with 1 tablespoon water
oil for deep-frying
200ml (7fl oz) ready-made lemon sauce *
slices of fresh lemon to garnish

Trim the chicken meat of fat. Marinate in the salt, pepper and wine for 25–30 minutes, then coat with the egg and flour paste.

Deep-fry the chicken pieces in hot oil (180°C/350°F) until golden brown. Remove and drain. Cut each breast into bite-sized pieces and arrange on a serving dish.

Heat about 1 tablespoon oil in a wok or saucepan and mix in the lemon sauce, blend well and pour evenly over the chicken. Garnish with lemon slices and serve hot.

*Lemon Sauce Ready-made lemon sauce in bottles is available from Oriental stores. Alternatively, it is not too difficult to make it at home:

1 tablespoon oil
200ml (1/3 pint) stock (see page 45)
1 tablespoon caster sugar
1 tablespoon lemon juice
1 tablespoon cornflour
1 teaspoon salt
pinch of MSG (optional)
1 teaspoon lemon rind

Heat the oil until hot, reduce the heat and add all the ingredients for the sauce, blend well and make smooth. Serve.

DEEP-FRIED SPARE-RIBS WITH SPICY SALT AND PEPPER
椒鹽排骨

Serves 4–6.

Preparation & cooking time: 45–50 mins & marinating & cooling time.

Ideally, the spare-ribs should be less than 15cm (6") long. In China, each rib is chopped into 3–4 bite-size pieces before or after cooking.

10–12 finger ribs, about 675g (1$^{1}/_{2}$lb) in weight
about 600ml (1 pint) stock (see page 45) or water
oil for deep-frying
1 teaspoon spicy salt and pepper (see page 83)

For the marinade:
$^{1}/_{2}$ teaspoon finely chopped garlic
1 tablespoon caster sugar
1 tablespoon light soy sauce
1 tablespoon dark soy sauce
2 tablespoons Chinese rice wine
$^{1}/_{2}$ teaspoon chilli sauce
a few drops of sesame oil
1 tablespoon cornflour

Trim off any excess fat and gristle from the ribs, marinate in the marinade for at least 2–3 hours, then add the stock or water and boil gently under cover for 35–40 minutes. Remove and drain, and leave to cool for 3–4 hours.

To cook: deep-fry the ribs in hot oil (190°C/375°F) for 2–3 minutes, remove and drain. Re-heat the oil and fry the ribs once more for another minute, or until dark brown. Remove and drain, and serve with spicy salt and pepper.

CRISPY SHREDDED BEEF
乾炒牛肉絲

Serves 4.

Preparation & cooking time: 25–30 mins.

350–400g (12–14oz) beefsteak (topside rump)
2 eggs, beaten
$^1/_2$ teaspoon salt
4–5 tablespoons cornflour
oil for deep-frying

For the sauce:
2 medium carrots, finely shredded
2 spring onions, thinly shredded
1–2 cloves garlic, finely chopped
2 fresh red or green chillies, seeded and thinly shredded*
4 tablespoons caster sugar
3 tablespoons rice vinegar
2 tablespoons light soy sauce

Thinly cut the beef into matchstick shreds. Make a batter with the eggs, salt and cornflour, then coat the shredded beef with this batter. Mix well.

Deep-fry the beef in hot oil (190°C/375°F) for 4–5 minutes, stir to separate the pieces, remove and drain. Deep-fry the carrots for 1¹/₂ minutes, pour off excess oil, leaving about 1 tablespoon in the wok or pan, add the spring onions, garlic and chilli, stir-fry for about 1 minute, now add the sugar, vinegar and soy sauce with the beef. Blend well so that each beef shred is coated with the sauce. Serve hot.

*Always handle fresh hot chillies with great care. See page 52.

SWEET AND SOUR PORK
香酥咕嚕肉

Serves 4.

Preparation & cooking: 35–40 mins & marinating.

One of the most popular dishes served in Chinese restaurants and take-aways in the West. Unfortunately, it's often spoiled by cooks who use too much tomato ketchup for the sauce.

350g (12oz) lean pork
salt and pepper to taste
1 tablespoon Chinese rice wine
1 egg, beaten
2 tablespoons plain flour
oil for deep-frying

For the sauce:
1 tablespoon oil
1 small onion, cut into small cubes
$^1/_2$ small green pepper, cut into small cubes
1 small carrot, cut into small cubes
1 tablespoon light soy sauce
2 tablespoons soft brown sugar
3 tablespoons rice vinegar
1 tablespoon tomato sauce (ketchup or purée)
$^1/_2$ teaspoon chilli sauce (optional)
about 100ml (4fl oz) stock or water
1 tablespoon thin cornflour paste (see page 40)

Cut the pork into small bite-size cubes (about the size of a walnut), and marinate in the salt, pepper and wine for 15–20 minutes. Coat the meat with the egg and flour, deep-fry in moderately hot oil (180°C/350°F) for about 3–4 minutes and stir it to separate the pieces. Remove and drain.

Reheat the oil and re-fry the meat for another minute or until golden brown. Remove and drain.

To make the sauce: heat the oil and add the vegetables, stir-fry for about 1 minute, then add the seasonings with the stock or water, bring to the boil and thicken with the cornflour paste. Now add the pork pieces, blending well so that each piece of the pork is coated with the sauce. Serve hot.

CRISPY-SKIN ('SMOKED') CHICKEN
脆皮炸子鷄

Serves 12–14 as a starter, or 4–6 as a main course.

Preparation & cooking time: 45–50 mins & marinating & cooling time.

Like the 'Smoked' Fish (on page 84), the chicken is not actually smoked.

It is not necessary to cook a whole chicken for this dish – use two half or four quarter portions, or at least 14 drumsticks if you prefer.

1 whole chicken, about 1.35kg (3lb)
about 1.2 litres (2 pints) 'Master Gravy' (see page 53)
2 tablespoons maltose or honey, dissolved with 3–4 tablespoons
    rice vinegar
oil for deep-frying
lettuce leaves to garnish

Clean the chicken well. Bring the 'Master Gravy' to a rolling boil and immerse the bird in it and simmer under cover for 25–30 minutes. Remove and brush it all over with the maltose or honey and vinegar solution while still hot, then hang it up to dry in a cool and airy place for at least 2–3 hours.

Deep-fry the chicken in hot oil (190°C/375°F) for 4–5 minutes or until golden brown, turning over constantly. Remove and drain.

To serve: chop the chicken through the bone (see pages 38–39) and arrange neatly on a bed of lettuce leaves.

6

ROASTED & BARBECUED DISHES

It is speculated that the earliest and most primitive method of cooking by our ancestors was a form of barbecuing – they simply baked the carcasses of animals on hot stones and ashes. Seasonings and other refinements, such as cutting the meat up into smaller pieces and cooking them on skewers, must have come much later. I mention this because I assume that the dietary habits of our ancestors probably did not differ greatly across the surface of the earth until the invention of different cooking utensils – and thereby different cooking methods and techniques.

Most home kitchens in China are only equipped with a stove, so the Chinese have to visit restaurants or take-aways to sample roasted and barbecued food; in fact, most take-aways in China sell only roasts and barbecues.

Since every home kitchen in the West has an oven, you should achieve high marks for these dishes: I would say a rating of 95%– 100% is not at all impossible!

ROASTED CRISPY PORK
五香燒腩

Serves 10–12 as a starter, or 6–8 as a main course.

Preparation & cooking time: about 1 hour & marinating time.

1kg (2¹/₄lb) belly of pork
2 teaspoons salt
2 teaspoons five-spice powder

For the dip:
3–4 tablespoons light soy sauce
1 tablespoon chilli sauce (optional)

Ideally, the pork should be in one piece. Dry the skin with kitchen paper and make sure that it is free from hairs. Rub the meat all over with the salt and five-spice powder, then leave to stand for at least 1 hour – longer if possible.

To cook: place the pork, skin side up, on a rack in a baking tin, and roast in a pre-heated oven (240°C/475°F/ Gas 9) for 20 minutes, then reduce the heat to 200°C/ 400°F/Gas 6, and cook for a further 40–45 minutes, or until the skin has become crackling.

To serve: chop the meat into small bite-size pieces, and serve hot or cold with the dip.

NB Any leftovers can be used in a number of dishes such as Mixed Meat Casserole (see page 216) and Assorted Meats and Rice (see page 226).

BARBECUED SPARE-RIBS
蜜汁燒排骨

Serves 10–12 as a starter, or 6–8 as a main course.

Preparation & cooking time: about 1 hour & marinating time.

The half saddle of pork spare-rib seen hanging in good Cantonese restaurants. (You can use individual ribs instead of a whole piece: cook them with the marinade and about 150ml (¹/₄ pint) water in a tin, ensuring the ribs are spread out and turned over at least once.)

1.1kg (2¹/₂lb) pork spare-ribs, in one piece

For the marinade:
2–3 cloves garlic, crushed
1 tablespoon crushed fresh ginger
1 teaspoon five-spice powder
1 tablespoon soft brown sugar
3 tablespoons brandy, whisky or rum
5 tablespoons light or dark soy sauce

Trim off and discard any excess fat and gristle from the ribs. Marinate the whole piece of the ribs in the marinade for 4–6 hours, turning or basting several times during the marinating.

To cook: fill a large roasting or baking tin with about 600ml (1 pint) boiling water, then place it on the bottom of an oven pre-heated to 230°C/450°F/Gas 8. Remove the spare-ribs from the marinade and insert two S-shaped meat hooks at each end of the ribs, and hang the whole piece from the highest rack in the oven directly above the tin of water.

Roast the ribs for 15–20 minutes, then baste with the marinade, reduce the heat to 200°C/400°F /Gas 6 and cook for 30–35 minutes more, or until the ribs are crisp and golden.

To serve: bring the marinade to the boil with the water and drippings from the baking tin, and thicken with a little cornflour to make a sauce. Cut the spare-ribs into individual ribs with a sharp knife; if you have a Chinese cleaver, then chop each rib into 3–4 bite-size pieces; pour some of the sauce over and serve hot.

CHAR SIU – HONEY ROASTED PORK
蜜汁叉燒

Serves 10–12 as a starter, or 6–8 as a main course.

Preparation & cooking time: about 35 mins & marinating time.

Also called Barbecued Pork in some restaurants, partly because of its reddish brown and slightly charred look around the edges.

1kg (2¹/₄lb) fillet of pork
2 tablespoons maltose or honey, dissolved with a little water

For the marinade:
1 tablespoon soft brown sugar
1 tablespoon yellow bean sauce
1 tablespoon light soy sauce
1 tablespoon dark soy sauce
1 tablespoon Hoi Sin sauce
1 tablespoon oyster sauce
2 tablespoons brandy, whisky or rum
1 teaspoon sesame oil

Cut the pork into strips about 4cm (1¹/₂") thick and 18–20cm (7–8") long, and marinate, covered, for at least 8–10 hours, turning occasionally.

To cook: preheat the oven to 220°C/425°F/Gas 7, and place a roasting or baking tin filled with about 600ml (1 pint) boiling water at the bottom. Take the pork strips out of the marinade, drain them well and reserve the marinade. Put the tip of an S-shaped hook through one end of each strip, then hang the strips on the top rack in the oven, making sure they dangle freely.

Roast for 10–15 minutes, then baste with the marinade, reduce the heat to 180°C/350°F /Gas 4, and cook for a further 8–10 minutes. Remove the meat from the oven, let it cool down for 2–3 minutes, then brush the strips with the maltose or honey syrup, and lightly brown them under a medium hot grill for 4–5 minutes, turning once or twice.

To serve: cut the meat across the grain into thin slices, and make a sauce by boiling the marinade and the water and drippings from the baking tin together for a few minutes, then strain into a gravy boat. Serve hot or cold.

ROAST DUCK – CANTONESE STYLE
脆皮燒鴨

Serves 10–12 as a starter, or 4–6 as a main course.

Preparation & cooking time: 1¹/₂ hours & drying time.

This is the duck with a shining reddish-brown skin seen hanging in the windows of a good Cantonese restaurant.

One 2kg (4¹/₂lb) oven-ready duckling
2 teaspoons salt
4 tablespoons maltose or honey
1 tablespoon rice vinegar
¹/₂ teaspoon red food colouring (optional)
about 280ml (¹/₂ pint) warm water

For the stuffing:
1 tablespoon oil
1 tablespoon finely chopped spring onions
1 teaspoon finely chopped fresh ginger root
1 tablespoon caster sugar
2 tablespoons Chinese rice wine
1 tablespoon yellow bean sauce
1 tablespoon Hoi Sin sauce
2 teaspoons five-spice powder

Clean the duck well. Remove the wing tips and the lumps of fat from inside the vent. Blanch in a pot of boiling water for a few minutes, remove and dry well, then rub the duck with salt, and tie the neck tightly with string.

Make the stuffing by heating the oil in a saucepan, add all the ingredients, bring to the boil and blend well. Pour the mixture into the cavity of the duck and sew it up securely.

Dissolve the maltose or honey with vinegar and red colouring (if using) in warm water, brush it all over the duck – give it several coatings, then hang the duck up (head down) with an S-shaped hook to dry in an airy and cool place for at least 4–5 hours.

To cook: preheat the oven to 200°C/400°F/Gas 6. Hang the duck head down on the top rack, and place a tray of boiling water at the bottom of the oven. Reduce the heat to 180°C/350°F /Gas 4, after 25 minutes or so, and cook for a further 30 minutes, basting with the remaining coating mixture once or twice.

To serve: let the duck cool down a little, then remove the string and pour out the liquid stuffing to be used as gravy. Chop the duck into bite-size pieces (see page 38–39), then serve hot or cold with the gravy poured over it.

PEKING DUCK
北京烤鴨

Serves 6–8.

Preparation & cooking time: 2 hours & drying time.

Strictly speaking, it is almost impossible to reproduce this dish at home in the West for two reasons. Firstly, the genuine article is a specially reared species of duck which is brought by several stages of force-feeding and care to exactly the right degree of plumpness and tenderness before it is prepared for the oven. Secondly, you are supposed to use a specially constructed kiln-like oven with Chinese date tree as fuel. But all is not lost, it is quite possible to prepare and cook this dish at home by following this recipe.

One 2.3–2.5kg (5–5^1/$_2$lb) oven-ready duckling
2 tablespoons maltose or honey, dissolved in 2 tablespoons water

For serving:
20–24 duck pancakes (see page 106)
100ml (4fl oz) duck sauce (see page 107) or plum sauce
6–8 spring onions, thinly shredded
^{1}/$_2$ cucumber, thinly shredded

Clean the duck well, remove the wing tips and any feather stubs, as well as the lumps of fat from inside the vent.

Plunge the duck into a pot of boiling water for 2–3 minutes. Remove and drain, dry thoroughly with kitchen paper. While the skin is still warm, brush the duck all over with the maltose or honey and water solution, then hang it up to dry in a cool and airy place for at least 4–5 hours or overnight.

To cook: place the duck, breast side up, on a rack in a roasting tin, and cook in an oven preheated to 200°C/400°F/Gas 6 for $1^1/_2$–$1^3/_4$ hours, without basting or turning.

To serve: peel off the crispy duck skin in small slices by using a sharp carving knife, then carve the meat into thin strips. Arrange the skin and meat on separate serving plates.

To eat: spread about 1 teaspoon of the sauce in the middle of a pancake, add a few strips of spring onions and cucumber, then top with 2–3 slices each of duck skin and meat. Roll up the pancake, turn up the bottom edge to prevent the contents from falling out. Eat with fingers.

Traditionally, the carcass of the duck is made into a delicious soup at the end of the meal (see page 69).

DUCK PANCAKES
鴨餅

Makes 24–30 pancakes.

Preparation & cooking time: about 1 hour & standing time.

Quite a lot of practice and patience is needed to achieve the perfect result. Most restaurants buy ready-made frozen ones from Chinese supermarkets.

450g (1lb) plain flour
about 300ml ($^1/_2$ pint) boiling water
1 teaspoon oil
dry flour for dusting

Sift the flour into a mixing bowl, pour in the water very gently, stir as you pour, then mix with the oil. Knead the mixture into a firm dough. Cover with a damp towel and let stand for about 30 minutes.

Lightly dust the surface of a worktop with dry flour; knead the dough for about 5–8 minutes or until smooth, then divide it into 3 equal portions. Roll out each portion into a long 'sausage', and cut each 'sausage' into 8–10 pieces.

Roll each piece into a ball, then, using the palm of your hand, press each piece into a flat pancake. Dust the surface with more flour, flatten each pancake into a 15cm (6") circle with a rolling pin and roll gently on both sides.

To cook: place an ungreased frying-pan over a high heat. When hot, reduce the heat to low and place the pancakes, one at a time, in the pan. Remove when little brown spots appear on the underside. Keep under a damp cloth until using.

DUCK SAUCE
鴨醬

1 tablespoon sesame oil
6–8 tablespoons yellow bean sauce
2 tablespoons caster sugar

Heat the sesame oil in a small saucepan, add the yellow bean sauce and sugar, stir to make smooth. Serve.

PORK/CHICKEN SATAY
猪肉／鷄肉串（沙爹）

Makes 24–26 sticks.

Preparation & cooking time: 20–25 mins & marinating time.

Small cubes of tender meat (pork, chicken, beef or lamb) are marinated in spices, then threaded onto bamboo skewers (satay sticks) and cooked on the barbecue or under the grill.

1lb (450g) pork fillet/chicken breast or thigh meat, etc
about 1 tablespoon vegetable oil
1 onion, cut into small cubes
$^1/_2$ cucumber, unpeeled and cubed
4–6 tablespoons satay sauce (see Glossary)

For the marinade:
1 teaspoon finely minced garlic
1 tablespoon finely minced shallots
2 tablespoons light soy sauce
1 tablespoon caster sugar
1 tablespoon coriander powder
1 tablespoon lemon juice or rice vinegar

Cut the meat into 2.5cm (1") cubes, and marinate in the marinade for at least 1 hour. Meanwhile, soak the bamboo satay sticks in water for about 30 minutes. Thread 3–4 meat cubes onto each bamboo satay stick.

To cook: brush each satay with a little oil and cook over a charcoal barbecue or under a hot grill for 6–8 minutes, turning frequently. Serve hot with onion, cucumber and satay sauce.

7

STEAMED DISHES

The main difference between Chinese steaming and Western steaming is that we place the food in a bowl or platter, or on a rack, uncovered, in a big steamer, which rests above plenty of boiling water inside a covered wok, so the food is cooked by intense hot steam under *and* around it. Fish and meat are sometimes marinated first, and they are usually served in the dish in which they were cooked.

The traditional Chinese steamer is made of bamboo. This imparts a subtle fragrance to the food, something I always find lacking in the food which has been cooked inside a modern aluminium steamer.

A wok can also be used as an improvised steamer: fill the wok about one-third full with water, bring to the boil, then place the food in a heatproof dish or bowl on a rack or trivet inside the wok and cover the wok with a dome-shaped lid.

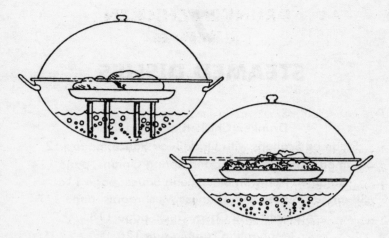

Fig. 22. Improvised steamers.
Upper: food is placed on a trivet.
Lower: food is placed on a rack.

The secret of successful steaming lies with the intensity of high heat and the quantity of water, which create the hot steam. The other point to remember is that the ingredients must be in prime condition – this is particularly important regarding fish and seafood.

DRUNKEN CHICKEN
酒蒸 (醉) 鷄

Serves 6–8 as a starter or 4–6 as a main meal.

Preparation & cooking time: about 2¹/₂ hours.

1 young chicken weighing about 1kg (2¹/₄lb)
2 teaspoons salt
150ml (¹/₄ pint) Chinese rice wine
3 tablespoons brandy, whisky or rum
1 tablespoon finely chopped fresh ginger root
2–3 spring onions, cut into short sections
salt and pepper to taste

Blanch the chicken in a pan of boiling water for 2–3 minutes. Remove it and place it (breast side down) in a large bowl, and add the salt, wine, spirit, ginger and spring onions. Place the bowl in a hot steamer and steam vigorously for at least 2 hours.

To serve: remove the chicken and place on a serving dish, breast side up. Adjust seasonings, pour the cooking liquid over the chicken and serve hot.

STEAMED SCALLOPS
WITH BLACK BEAN SAUCE
清蒸鮮貝

Serves 6–8 as a starter.

Preparation & cooking time: 10–15 mins.

Fresh scallops in their shells are quite expensive and not that easy to
come by, but it is worth your while to track them down as they make
an excellent starter – and the shells make decorative ornaments.

12 fresh scallops in their shells

For the sauce:
2 tablespoons oil
$^1/_2$ teaspoon finely chopped garlic
$^1/_2$ teaspoon finely chopped fresh ginger root
1 tablespoon finely chopped spring onions
1 teaspoon finely chopped fresh red or green chilli*
1 tablespoon light soy sauce
1 tablespoon Chinese rice wine
2 tablespoons black bean sauce
2 tablespoons stock (see page 45)
a few drops of sesame oil

Scrub the scallops under running cold water, then open them and discard the flat half of each shell. Prise off the flesh but leave it in the shell.

To cook: place the scallops in their shells on a large heatproof dish in a hot steamer and steam for 8–9 minutes over a high heat. Meanwhile, heat the oil in a wok or small saucepan, add the garlic, ginger, spring onions and chilli, stir-fry for 30 seconds, then add the rest of the ingredients, blend well, bring to the boil, and simmer for about 1 minute.

To serve: pour about 2 teaspoons of the sauce over each scallop and serve them in the shells. The flesh can easily be removed from the shell with a pair of chopsticks or a fork.

*NB Handle fresh chillies with great care. See page 52.

STEAMED FISH WITH GINGER AND SPRING ONIONS
清蒸海上鮮

Serves 4–6.

Preparation & cooking time: 25–30 mins.

Most restaurants offer either sea bass or Dover sole on their menu for this dish – neither is cheap, however delicious they might be. I suggest that you use a trout, grey mullet, lemon sole or whiting for this recipe.

1 whole fish (sea bass, trout or grey mullet, etc) weighing about 675g (1$^1/_2$lb), cleaned

$^1/_2$ teaspoon salt

1 teaspoon sesame oil

4 spring onions

2–3 dried Chinese mushrooms (see Glossary), soaked and shredded (optional)

50g (2oz) pork fillet, thinly shredded (optional)

2 tablespoons light soy sauce

1 tablespoon Chinese rice wine

1 tablespoon thinly shredded fresh ginger root

2 tablespoons oil

Make sure the fish is scaled and gutted. Wash and dry it well both inside and out with a cloth or kitchen paper. Score both sides of the fish diagonally as far as the bone at intervals of 2.5cm (about 1"). Rub the salt and sesame oil inside and outside the fish, and place it on top of 2–3 spring onions on a platter.

Mix the mushrooms and pork (if using) with a little of the soy sauce and wine. Stuff about half of this mixture inside the fish and place the rest on top with the ginger. Place the platter in a hot steamer and steam over a high heat for 15 minutes.

Meanwhile, thinly shred the remaining spring onions. Heat the oil in a little saucepan until bubbling. Remove the fish from the steamer, arrange the spring onion shreds on top, pour the remaining soy sauce and wine over it, then pour the hot oil over the whole length of the fish. Serve hot.

STEAMED FISH WITH BLACK BEAN SAUCE
豉汁蒸魚

Serves 4.

Preparation & cooking time: 20–25 mins.

There is very little difference in the cooking methods for this dish and for the previous one – except this recipe is more suitable for cooking a flat fish or fish steaks rather than a whole round fish.

4 salmon steaks, weighing about 115-175g (4–6oz) each
$1/2$ teaspoon salt
1 teaspoon sesame oil
2 spring onions, cut in half lengthways
2 tablespoons black bean sauce
1 tablespoon light soy sauce
1 tablespoon Chinese rice wine
1 tablespoon finely shredded fresh ginger root
1 tablespoon oil
fresh coriander leaves to garnish

Rub both sides of the fish with salt and sesame oil, then place the fish on top of the spring onions in a heat-proof dish. Blend the black bean sauce with the soy sauce, wine and ginger, and pour evenly all over the fish. Place the dish in a hot steamer or inside a wok on a rack, and steam over a high heat for 12–15 minutes.

Heat the oil until hot. Remove the dish from the steamer and pour the hot oil all over the fish steaks. Garnish with coriander leaves and serve hot.

STEAMED CHICKEN WITH CHINESE MUSHROOMS
清蒸滑鷄

Serves 4–6

Preparation & cooking time: 25–30 mins & marinating time.

The chicken should be chopped through the bone into small bite-size pieces. Use thighs and drumsticks rather than breasts for this dish.

675g (1¹/₂lb) chicken meat
1 teaspoon caster sugar
1 tablespoon light soy sauce
1 tablespoon Chinese rice wine
2 teaspoons cornflour
3–4 dried Chinese mushrooms, soaked (see Glossary)
1 tablespoon finely shredded fresh ginger root
salt and pepper to taste
sesame oil to garnish (optional)

Chop the chicken through the bone into small bite-size pieces and marinate in the sugar, soy sauce, wine and cornflour for 25–30 minutes. Squeeze dry the mushrooms, discard any hard stalks and thinly shred.

Place the chicken pieces on a heat-proof plate, arrange the mushroom and ginger shreds on top. Garnish with salt and pepper and sesame oil. Place the plate on the rack inside a hot steamer and cook over a high heat for 20 minutes. Serve hot.

AROMATIC AND CRISPY DUCK
香酥鴨

Serves 10–12 as a starter, or 6–8 as a main course.

Preparation & cooking time: about 6–8 hours & marinating & cooling time.

Because this dish is served with spring onions, cucumber and a sweetish bean sauce wrapped in pancakes, many people mistakenly believe this is *the* Peking duck, which though crispy, is not so aromatic (see page 104).

One 2.3kg (5lb) oven-ready duckling
2 teaspoons salt
oil for deep-frying

For the marinade:
5–6 star anise pieces
1 tablespoon Sichuan red peppercorns
1 teaspoon cloves
2–3 cinnamon sticks
3–4 spring onions
3–4 pieces fresh ginger root, unpeeled
5–6 tablespoons Chinese rice wine

For serving:
20–24 duck pancakes (see page 106)
6–8 spring onions, thinly shredded
$^1/_2$ cucumber, thinly shredded
100ml (4fl oz) duck sauce (see page 107) or plum sauce (see Glossary)

Remove the wing tips and the lumps of fat from inside the vent. Split the duck in half down the backbone. Rub the salt all over both sides, and marinate in a dish with the marinade for at least 4–6 hours, turning several times.

Steam the duck pieces (skin-side up) with the marinade in a hot steamer over a high heat for at least 3–4 hours – have a kettle of boiling water ready to replenish when necessary. Remove from the cooking liquid and leave to cool for at least 6–8 hours – this is very important, for unless the duck is cold and dry, the skin will not be crispy.

To serve: deep-fry the duck pieces, skin-side down for 6–8 minutes or until crisp and brown, turning once in the last minute. Remove and drain.

To eat: scrape the meat from the bone and wrap it in the pancakes with strips of spring onions, cucumber and duck or plum sauce as when eating the Peking Duck (see page 104), or alternatively, use crispy lettuce leaves (Webb or Iceberg) instead of the pancakes.

MONGOLIAN LAMB
羊肉包

Serves 6–8.

Preparation & cooking time: about 3 hours & marinating & cooling time.

Also known as Mongolian Barbecued Lamb, the cooking method is in fact almost identical to that used for Aromatic and Crispy Duck (see page 118).

1.25kg (2¹/₂–2³/₄lb) leg of lamb fillet, boneless
oil for deep-frying

For the marinade:
2 teaspoons finely chopped fresh ginger root
1 tablespoon finely chopped spring onions
2 teaspoons ground Sichuan red peppercorns
2 teaspoons salt
2 tablespoons light soy sauce
1 tablespoon yellow bean sauce
1 tablespoon Hoi Sin sauce
1 teaspoon five-spice powder
2 tablespoons Chinese rice wine

For serving:
crisp lettuce leaves (Webb or Iceberg)
8–10 tablespoons duck sauce (see page 107)
¹/₂ finely shredded cucumber
6–8 finely shredded spring onions

Cut the lamb along the grain into 6 long strips. Marinate in the marinade for at least 2 hours. Pack the lamb with the marinade in a heat-proof dish or bowl, steam in a hot steamer over a high heat for 2–3 hours. Remove and leave to cool.

Take the meat out of the bowl and drain. Deep-fry in hot oil for 3–4 minutes. Cut the lamb into bite-size pieces.

To serve, place about 1 tablespoon of the lamb in the middle of a lettuce leaf, then about 1 teaspoon of the sauce and a few shreds of cucumber and spring onions. Roll up tightly to form a small parcel and eat with fingers.

STEAMED PORK SPARE-RIBS WITH BLACK BEAN SAUCE
豉汁蒸排骨

Serves 4–6.

Preparation & cooking time: 35–40 mins & marinating time.

A delicious Cantonese dish, and very simple to prepare.

450g (1lb) pork spare-ribs
2 spring onions, cut into short sections, to garnish

For the marinade:
1 teaspoon finely chopped garlic
$^1/_2$ teaspoon finely chopped fresh ginger root
1 teaspoon finely chopped fresh red or green chillies*
2 tablespoons black bean sauce
1 tablespoon light soy sauce
1 tablespoon Chinese rice wine
2 teaspoons cornflour

Chop the spare-ribs into small bite-size pieces, marinate in the marinade for at least 1 hour – the longer the better.

To cook: spread the ribs out on a heat-proof platter, steam in a hot steamer over a high heat for 25–30 minutes. Remove the platter and serve hot with the garnish.

***NB** Handle fresh chillies with great care. See page 52.

8

STIR-FRIED DISHES

See Also:

Chow Mein (Fried Noodles) and Fried Rice, etc in Chapter 12.

Stir-frying (CHAO) is by far the most frequently used cooking method in China. It's quick and simple: the actual cooking time usually takes no more than a few minutes, provided all the preparations are done beforehand.

Basically, a small amount of oil is healed in a wok, then the ingredients are added to be stirred and tossed with seasonings for a short while. Nothing could be simpler, but – and this is a big but – what most cookery writers fail to say is that first of all, the wok must be heated to a high degree before the oil is added, and furthermore, the oil should not only be seasoned, but also preheated just before being added to the wok used for stir-frying (see page 44).

There are many variations of stir-frying, the following are some of the most commonly used methods;

(a) **Pure Stir-frying**: the ingredients are not marinated nor coated with a batter – they are just stir-fried in hot oil, and seasonings are added towards the end of cooking.

(b) **Soft Stir-frying**: the main and supplementary ingredients are stir-fried separately and are brought together with the addition of seasonings and a thickening agent.

(c) **Twice Cooked Stir-frying**: one ingredient has been previously cooked and is then cut into smaller pieces and stir-fried with the other ingredients and seasonings.

The two most important points in any type of cooking – particularly for stir-frying the Chinese way – are the temperature of the heat and the timing.

A Chinese cook uses all five senses – sight, sound, taste, touch and smell – while preparing food. The sound of the sizzle when food is added to the preheated wok is important: it indicates instantly whether the preheated wok and oil are at the correct temperatures – something Western cooks need not worry too much about, since they can always rely on gadgets such as automatic controls, thermometers, regulators and other timing devices to guide them. All this is fine when cooking in an oven or in a deep-fat fryer with automatic control, or with a thermometer clipped to the side of the frying pan, but none of these devices will work when it comes to stir-frying. Here you just have to rely entirely on your intuition – use your eyes, nose, ears, hands and mind to judge whether the temperatures are correct, or the amount of seasoning is just right, and the timing is spot on.

Of course, all these skills require long experience, so do not expect too high a success rating to start with. I would say that an 85% mark would be a great achievement. Remember that the gas burners in a Chinese restaurant kitchen have been specially converted to give extra intense heat – something you can never hope to match at home. Nevertheless, not all stir-fried dishes require intense heat, therefore you should be able to obtain a 100% mark on certain dishes – maybe after a few attempts!

STIR-FRIED PRAWNS WITH MANGE-TOUT
蝦仁炒雪豆

Serves 4.

Preparation & cooking time: 20–25 mins.

This is a very colourful and delicious dish – the mange-tout can be substituted or supplemented with other vegetables.

170–225g (6–8oz) uncooked prawns
1 teaspoon salt
$^1/_3$ egg white
2 teaspoons thick cornflour paste (see page 40)
170g (6oz) mange-tout
1 small carrot
about 300ml ($^1/_2$ pint) seasoned oil (see page 44)
1 spring onion, cut into short sections
a few small bits of peeled fresh ginger root
$^1/_2$ teaspoon soft brown sugar
1 tablespoon light soy sauce
1 teaspoon Chinese rice wine
pinch of MSG (optional)
a few drops of sesame oil

Shell and de-vein the prawns, mix with a pinch of the salt, egg white and cornflour paste.

Top and tail the mange-tout, and cut the carrot into small, thin slices about the same size as the mange-tout.

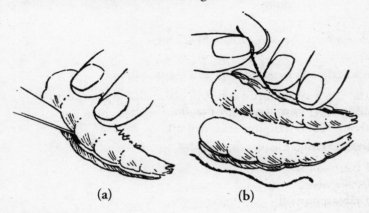

(a)   (b)

Fig. 23. De-veining prawns.
(a) Holding the tails, make a shallow cut, three-quarters of the way down, along the centre of the prawn's back.
(b) Pull out or scrape and discard the black or dark brown vein from the shallow cut.

To cook: heat a wok over a high heat for 2–3 minutes, then add a small amount of preheated oil to grease the wok, stirring with a stirrer so that about three-quarters of the surface of the wok is greased. Now add the rest of the oil (which should not be cold, but still quite warm), followed by the prawns to be blanched for about 30 seconds or until their colour changes. Remove the prawns with a strainer and drain.

Pour off the excess oil leaving about 1 tablespoon in the wok. Add the vegetables and stir-fry for about 1–1$\frac{1}{2}$ minutes, then add the remaining salt and sugar followed by the prawns. Stir for a few more times, then add the soy sauce, wine and MSG (if using). Blend well, finally add the sesame oil and serve.

SICHUAN PRAWNS
乾燒明蝦

Serves 4.

Preparation & cooking time: 20–25 mins.

Also called Prawns in Chilli and Garlic Sauce.

225g (8oz) uncooked tiger prawns
about 300ml (¹/₂ pint) seasoned oil
fresh coriander leaves to garnish

For the sauce:
1 tablespoon oil
3–4 small dried red chillies, soaked in warm water for 10 minutes,
    then deseeded and finely chopped
¹/₂ teaspoon finely chopped garlic
¹/₂ teaspoon finely chopped fresh ginger root
1 tablespoon light soy sauce
1 tablespoon Chinese rice wine
1 tablespoon chilli bean sauce
1 teaspoon tomato purée (NB not ketchup)
about 3 tablespoons stock (see page 45)
1 tablespoon finely chopped spring onions
a few drops of sesame oil
2 teaspoons thin cornflour paste (see page 40)

Remove the legs and tails of the prawns by pulling them off with your fingers, but leave the body shells on. De-vein them (see page 127) and pat dry with kitchen paper. Heat the seasoned oil in a preheated wok, then blanch the prawns in it for about 1 minute at the most or until they turn bright pink. Quickly remove them with a strainer and drain.

Pour off the oil and wipe clean the wok. Add the tablespoon of fresh oil and heat until hot. Now add the chillies, garlic and ginger to flavour the oil for a few seconds, then add the blanched prawns and stir-fry for about 30–40 seconds, then add the soy sauce, wine, chilli bean sauce, tomato paste and stock, blend well and bring to the boil. Braise for about 1 minute, stirring constantly, then add the spring onions and sesame oil, and thicken the sauce with the cornflour paste. Garnish and serve hot.

STIR-FRIED SCALLOPS WITH VEGETABLES
時菜炒帶子

Serves 4.

Preparation & cooking time: 25–30 mins.

Fresh scallops without their shells are quite inexpensive. But remember that the delicate flavour and texture will be lost if you overcook them.

6–8 fresh scallops
$1/4$ egg white
2 teaspoons thick cornflour paste (see page 40)
about 300ml ($1/2$ pint) seasoned oil (see page 44)
1 spring onion, cut into short sections
3–4 small bits of fresh ginger root
50g (2oz) Chinese leaves, cut into small pieces
25g (1oz) carrot, thinly sliced
25g (1oz) mange-tout, topped and tailed
50g (2oz) baby corn cobs, halved
50g (2oz) straw mushrooms, halved
1 teaspoon salt
$1/2$ teaspoon soft brown sugar
1 tablespoon light soy sauce
2 teaspoons Chinese rice wine
pinch of MSG (optional)
a few drops of sesame oil

Cut each scallop into 3–4 slices, and mix with the egg white and cornflour paste. Heat the oil in a preheated wok. Blanch the prawns for about 1 minute, then remove with a strainer and drain.

Pour off the excess oil, leaving about 1 tablespoon in the wok. Add the spring onion and ginger to flavour the oil for a few seconds, then stir-fry all the vegetables for 1–2 minutes. Now add the salt and sugar, continue stirring for 30 seconds, then add the scallops, followed by the soy sauce and wine; blend well for about 30 seconds. Finally add the MSG (if using) and the sesame oil, stir for a few more seconds, and serve hot.

MIXED SEAFOOD WITH VEGETABLES
三鮮炒時菜

Serves 4–6.

Preparation & cooking time: about 30–35 mins.

It is not necessary to use all the different ingredients for this dish – either of the two shellfish can be omitted.

115–175g (4–6oz) cleaned squid
115g (4oz) uncooked prawns
3–4 fresh scallops
$1/3$ egg white
1 tablespoon thick cornflour paste (see page 40)
about 300ml ($1/2$ pint) seasoned oil (see page 44)
$1/2$ teaspoon finely chopped fresh ginger root
1–2 spring onions, cut into short sections
2–3 stalks of celery, thinly sliced diagonally
1 small carrot, thinly sliced diagonally
1 small red pepper, cored, seeded, cut into small pieces
1 teaspoon salt
$1/2$ teaspoon soft brown sugar
1 tablespoon light soy sauce
1 tablespoon Chinese rice wine
about 2 tablespoons stock (see page 45)
a few drops of sesame oil

Prepare and blanch the squid as for Deep-Fried Squid on page 82. Shell and de-vein the prawns (see page 127), then cut each one in half lengthways. Cut each scallop into 3–4 slices. Mix the prawns and scallops with the egg white and half of the cornflour paste.

Heat the oil in a preheated wok until medium hot, then blanch the seafood for about 30–40 seconds, remove and drain.

Pour off the excess oil, leaving about 2 tablespoons in the wok, add the ginger and spring onions to flavour the oil first, then add the vegetables, stir-fry for about 1 minute, and add the salt and sugar. Continue stirring for another minute, then add the seafood, soy sauce and wine, blend well and add the stock; thicken this gravy with the remaining cornflour paste, add the sesame oil and serve hot.

MINCED CHICKEN SERVED WITH LETTUCE LEAVES
生菜包

Serves 4–6.

Preparation & cooking time: about 35–40 mins.

The original version of this recipe uses quail or pigeon meat. Some restaurants use pork instead of chicken.

225–275g (8–10oz) chicken thigh meat (boned and skinned)
salt and pepper to taste
$^1/_2$ teaspoon caster sugar
1 teaspoon light soy sauce
1 teaspoon Chinese rice wine
1 teaspoon thick cornflour paste (see page 40)
6 small dried Chinese mushrooms, soaked (see Glossary)
50g (2oz) Szechwan Preserved Vegetables (see Glossary), rinsed
50g (2oz) water chestnuts, drained and rinsed
4 tablespoons seasoned oil (see page 44)
$^1/_2$ teaspoon finely chopped fresh ginger root
1 tablespoon finely chopped spring onions
2 tablespoons oyster sauce
12 crisp (Webb or Iceberg) lettuce leaves to serve

Coarsely mince or chop the chicken meat, and marinate in the salt, pepper, sugar, soy sauce, wine and cornflour paste for 10–15 minutes.

Squeeze dry the mushrooms and discard any hard stalks. Coarsely chop the mushrooms, Preserved Vegetables and water chestnuts.

Heat the oil in a preheated wok, add the ginger and spring onions first, then the chicken, and stir-fry for about 1 minute. Now add all three vegetables; continue stirring for 2 minutes, then add the oyster sauce, blend well and cook for 1 more minute.

Serve hot. Place about 2–3 tablespoons of the mixture onto a lettuce leaf and roll it up tightly. Eat with your fingers.

UNG-PO CHICKEN
WITH CASHEW NUTS

宮保腰果鷄丁

Serves 4.

Preparation & cooking time: about 25–30 mins.

Kung-Po was a Court Official in Sichuan, and this very popular dish
was created by his cook. Peanuts were used instead of cashew nuts in
the original version.

275–350g (10–12oz) boned, skinned chicken thigh meat
pinch of salt
^{1}/$_4$ egg white
2 teaspoons thick cornflour paste (see page 40)
about 300ml (^{1}/$_2$ pint) seasoned oil (see page 44)
3–4 small dried red chillies, soaked and seeded, chopped
a few small bits of fresh ginger root
1 spring onion, cut into short sections
1 green pepper, cored, seeded, cut into small pieces
1 tablespoon yellow bean sauce
1 teaspoon chilli bean sauce
2 teaspoons Chinese rice wine
a pinch of MSG (optional)
85g (3oz) roasted cashew nuts
a few drops of sesame oil

Cut the chicken meat into small cubes about the size of sugar lumps, and mix with the salt, egg white and cornflour paste.

Heat the oil in a preheated wok, blanch the chicken cubes for about 1 minute, stirring to separate the cubes, then remove and drain them.

Pour off the excess oil, leaving about 1 tablespoon in the wok, add the chillies, ginger and spring onion followed by the green pepper, stir-fry for about 1 minute, then add the yellow and chilli bean sauces, cook for 30 seconds, now add the chicken cubes with the wine, and blend well. Finally add the MSG (if using), cashew nuts and sesame oil, stir a few times and serve hot.

(Omit the dried chillies and the chilli bean sauce to make Stir-fried Diced Chicken with Cashew Nuts.)

CHICKEN WITH BAMBOO SHOOTS AND MUSHROOMS
雙冬鷄片

Serves 4.

Preparation & cooking time: about 20–25 mins.

225g (8oz) chicken breast fillet
1 teaspoon salt
¼ egg white
2 teaspoons thick cornflour paste (see page 40)
8–10 small dried Chinese mushrooms, soaked (see Glossary)
about 300ml (½ pint) seasoned oil (see page 44)
1 spring onion, cut into short sections
a few small bits of fresh ginger root
115–175g (4–6oz) sliced bamboo shoots, rinsed and drained
½ teaspoon soft brown sugar
1 tablespoon light soy sauce
1 tablespoon oyster sauce
2 teaspoons Chinese rice wine
a pinch of MSG (optional)
a few drops of sesame oil

Cut the chicken into thin slices about the size of large postage stamps, and mix with a pinch of the salt, and the egg white and the cornflour paste. Squeeze dry the mushrooms and discard any hard stalks.

Heat the oil in a preheated wok, blanch the chicken slices for about 30 seconds, stirring to separate them, then remove and drain them.

Pour off the excess oil, leaving about 2 tablespoons in the wok, add the spring onion and ginger, followed by the mushrooms and bamboo shoots, stir-fry for about 1 minute, then add the remaining salt and sugar, continue stirring for another minute or so, then add the chicken slices, and blend well; now add the soy sauce, oyster sauce and wine, and stir-fry for another minute. Finally add the MSG, if using, and the sesame oil. Serve hot.

SHREDDED CHICKEN WITH VEGETABLES
鷄絲炒時菜

Serves 4.

Preparation & cooking time: about 25–30 mins.

This is the classical 'Chicken Chop Suey' dish that heralded Chinese food to the Western world at the end of the 19th century – it is rather amazing to think that one of the world's greatest cuisines should have been represented by a dish that did not even originate in China itself, but thousands of miles away in San Francisco, USA!

115–175g (4–6oz) chicken meat, thinly shredded
1 teaspoon salt
$^1/_4$ egg white
1 tablespoon thick cornflour paste (see page 40)
about 300ml ($^1/_2$ pint) seasoned oil (see page 44)
$^1/_2$ teaspoon finely chopped garlic (optional)
1 tablespoon thinly shredded fresh ginger root
3–4 spring onions, thinly shredded
115–175g (4–6oz) bean sprouts
1 small green pepper, cored and seeded, thinly shredded
$^1/_2$ teaspoon caster sugar
1 tablespoon light soy sauce
$^1/_2$ tablespoon Chinese rice wine
2 tablespoons stock (see page 45)
pinch of MSG (optional)
a few drops of sesame oil

Mix the chicken shreds with a pinch of the salt, the egg white and about 1 *teaspoon* cornflour paste. Blanch them in warm oil, stir to separate, then remove and drain them.

Pour off the excess oil, leaving about 2 tablespoons in the wok, stir-fry all the vegetables for about 1 minute, add the remaining salt and sugar, blend well, then add the chicken with the soy sauce and wine, stir-fry for another minute, and add the stock and MSG, if using; finally thicken the gravy with the remaining cornflour paste, garnish with the sesame oil and serve hot.

STIR-FRIED PORK WITH VEGETABLES
時菜肉片

Serves 4.

Preparation & cooking time: about 25–30 mins.

A basic 'meat and veg' recipe – the meat and vegetables can be varied according to seasonal availability.

225g (8oz) pork fillet
1 teaspoon soft brown sugar
1 teaspoon light soy sauce
1 teaspoon Chinese rice wine
2 teaspoons thick cornflour paste (see page 40)
5–6 small dried Chinese mushrooms, soaked (see Glossary)
about 300ml (¹/₂ pint) seasoned oil (see page 44)
a few small bits of fresh ginger root
1 spring onion, cut into short sections
50g (2oz) sliced bamboo shoots, rinsed and drained
50g (2oz) Chinese leaves, cut into small pieces
50g (2oz) mange-tout, topped and tailed
1 teaspoon salt
1 tablespoon oyster sauce
2 tablespoons stock (see page 45)
pinch of MSG (optional)
a few drops of sesame oil

Cut the pork into thin slices about the size of a large postage stamp, marinate in $1/2$ teaspoon sugar, the soy sauce, wine and 1 teaspoon cornflour paste for 10–15 minutes. Squeeze dry the mushrooms and discard any hard stalks.

Heat the oil in a preheated wok and blanch the pork for about 1 minute, or until the colour changes, then remove and drain.

Pour off the excess oil, leaving about 2 tablespoons in the wok. Add the ginger and spring onion to flavour the oil first, then stir-fry the vegetables for about 2 minutes, add the salt and the remaining sugar, blend well, then add the pork and oyster sauce with the stock, bring to the boil, cook for 1 more minute and add the MSG, if using; finally thicken the gravy with the remaining cornflour paste, garnish with the sesame oil and serve hot.

STIR-FRIED SQUID WITH CHILLI AND BLACK BEAN SAUCE

豉椒鮮魷

Serves 4.

Preparation & cooking time: 35–40 mins.

350–400g (12–14oz) cleaned squid
1 small onion
1 small green pepper, cored and seeded
3–4 tablespoons seasoned oil (see page 44)
3–4 small bits of fresh ginger root
1 spring onion, cut into short sections
1–2 fresh green chillies, cut into small bits*
2 tablespoons black bean sauce
1 tablespoon Chinese rice wine
a few drops of sesame oil

Prepare and blanch the squid as described on page 82 for Deep-fried Squid.

Cut the onion and green pepper into small triangular pieces. Heat the oil in a preheated wok until smoking, then add the ginger, spring onion and chillies, followed by the onion and green pepper; stir-fry for about 1 minute, then add the black bean sauce, stir for another minute before adding the squid with the wine, and blend well. Finally add the sesame oil and serve hot.

*NB Handle fresh chillies with great care. See page 52.

TWICE-COOKED PORK
回鍋肉

Serves 4.

Preparation & cooking time: 20–25 mins & extra pre-cooking time if using fresh meat.

Any leftovers from 'White-Cut' Pork (see page 49) can be used for this dish instead of using fresh meat.

175g (6oz) ready-cooked pork, or 275g (10oz) fresh pork
3 tablespoons seasoned oil (see page 44)
1 spring onion, cut into short sections
1 small green pepper, cored and seeded, cut into small slices
115g (4oz) sliced bamboo shoots, rinsed and drained
1 teaspoon salt
$^1/_2$ teaspoon soft brown sugar
1 tablespoon yellow bean sauce
2 teaspoons chilli bean sauce
2 teaspoons Chinese rice wine
pinch of MSG (optional)
a few drops of sesame oil

If no ready-cooked pork is available, then cook the piece of fresh pork by simmering it in a pot of boiling water for 20–25 minutes under cover, then turn off the heat and leave it in the water for at least 2–3 hours before removing it to cool. Cut the pork into thin slices about the size of a large postage stamp.

Heat the oil in a preheated wok until smoking, stir-fry the vegetables for about 1 minute, then add the pork with the salt, sugar, yellow and chilli bean sauces and wine, blend well and cook for another minute; finally add the MSG, if using, and the sesame oil; stir a few more times and serve hot.

MU-SHU PORK
(SERVED WITH PANCAKES)
木須肉絲

Serves 4.

Preparation & cooking time: 25–30 mins.

Sometimes listed as 'Mou-Shou Rou' or 'Moo-Shoo Pork', or just 'Shredded Pork with Scrambled Egg' – *mu shu* being the Chinese name for a bright yellow flower with the colour of scrambled eggs.

10g (¹/₄oz) dried black fungus (wood ears, see Glossary)
170–225g (6–8oz) pork fillet
50g (2oz) bamboo shoots, rinsed and drained
115g (4oz) Chinese leaves
3 eggs, beaten
1 teaspoon salt
4 tablespoons seasoned oil (see page 44)
2 spring onions, thinly shredded
1 tablespoon light soy sauce
2 teaspoons Chinese rice wine
pinch of MSG (optional)
a few drops of sesame oil
12 duck pancakes (see page 106) to serve

Soak the wood ears in warm water for 15–20 minutes, rinse and drain, then thinly shred. Cut the pork, bamboo shoots and Chinese leaves all into matchstick-sized shreds.

Beat the eggs with a pinch of salt. Heat about 1 tablespoon oil in a preheated wok and scramble the eggs until set. Remove from the wok onto a plate.

Heat the remaining oil until hot, stir-fry the pork shreds for about 1 minute or until the colour changes, then add the shredded vegetables, stir-fry for another minute or so, now add the remaining salt, soy sauce and wine, and blend well before adding the scrambled eggs, stirring to break them into small bits; finally add MSG (if using) and the sesame oil, stir a few times more and serve hot.

To eat: put about 2 tablespoons Mu-Shu Pork in the centre of a warmed pancake, roll it into a parcel and turn up the bottom end to prevent the contents from falling out. Eat with your fingers.

STIR-FRIED BEEF WITH OYSTER SAUCE
蠔油牛肉

Serves 4.

Preparation & cooking: 25–30 mins & marinating.

Have you ever wondered how Chinese chefs can always cook a beef dish to such perfection with tender meat full of flavour? The secret is to use an inexpensive cut of beef, to marinate in a special marinade, and finish off with oyster sauce.

275–350g (10–12oz) beefsteak, such as topside rump
4–6 small dried Chinese mushrooms, soaked (see Glossary)
about 600ml (1 pint) seasoned oil (see page 44)
a few small bits of fresh ginger root
1 spring onion, cut into short sections
115g (4oz) mange-tout, topped and tailed
$^1/_2$ small carrot, thinly sliced
$^1/_2$ teaspoon salt
$^1/_2$ teaspoon soft brown sugar
2 tablespoons oyster sauce

For the marinade:
$^1/_2$ teaspoon soft brown sugar
1 tablespoon dark or light soy sauce
2 teaspoons Chinese rice wine
$^1/_2$ teaspoon bicarbonate of soda or baking powder
2 teaspoons thick cornflour paste (see page 40)
1 tablespoon oil

Cut the beef across the grain into thin slices about the size of a large postage stamp, and marinate in the marinade for several hours – overnight if possible. Squeeze dry the mushrooms and discard any hard stalks.

Heat the oil in a preheated wok until medium hot, blanch the beef for about 40–50 seconds, stir to separate the slices, then remove as soon as the colour changes. Drain.

Pour off the excess oil, leaving about 2 tablespoons in the wok, stir-fry the vegetables for 1 minute, add the salt and sugar, continue stirring for another minute, then add the beef and the oyster sauce, blend well and serve hot.

STIR-FRIED BEEF WITH CHILLI AND BLACK BEAN SAUCE
豉椒牛肉

Serves 4.

Preparation & cooking time: 20–25 mins & marinating time.

275–350g (10–12oz) beefsteak, such as topside rump
1 small onion
1 small green pepper, cored and seeded
about 600ml (1 pint) seasoned oil (see page 44)
a few small bits of fresh ginger root
1 spring onion, cut into short sections
1–2 fresh red or green chillies, cut into small bits*
2 tablespoons black bean sauce
pinch of MSG (optional)

For the marinade:
$^1/_2$ teaspoon soft brown sugar
1 tablespoon dark or light soy sauce
2 teaspoons Chinese rice wine
$^1/_2$ teaspoon bicarbonate of soda or baking powder
2 teaspoons thick cornflour paste (see page 40)
1 tablespoon oil

Cut the beef into thin slices about the size of large postage stamps. Marinate in the marinade for at least 2–3 hours.

Cut the onion and green pepper into small triangular pieces. Heat the oil in a preheated wok until medium hot, blanch the beef for about 1 minute or until the colour changes, stirring to separate the slices; remove with a strainer and drain.

Pour off the excess oil, leaving about 2 tablespoons in the wok, add the ginger and spring onion to flavour the oil for a few seconds, then stir-fry the chillies, onion and green pepper for about 1 minute; now add the black bean sauce, and cook for another minute before adding the beef, blend well; finally add the MSG (if using), stir a few times more and serve hot.

*NB Handle fresh chillies with great care. See page 52.

FILLET BEEF CANTONESE STYLE
中式牛柳

Serves 4.

Preparation & cooking time: 10–15 mins & marinating time.

Again, do not use the expensive cuts of beef steak.

8 minute beef steaks, each weighing about 50g (2oz)
about 300ml ($^1/_2$ pint) seasoned oil (see page 44)
finely chopped spring onion to garnish

For the marinade:
$^1/_2$ teaspoon soft brown sugar
1 tablespoon dark or light soy sauce
2 teaspoons Chinese rice wine
$^1/_2$ teaspoon bicarbonate of soda or baking powder
2 teaspoons thick cornflour paste (see page 40)
1 tablespoon oil

For the sauce:
$^1/_2$ teaspoon finely chopped garlic
$^1/_2$ teaspoon finely chopped fresh ginger root
1 teaspoon soft brown sugar
1 tablespoon light soy sauce
2 tablespoons Worcester sauce
about 150ml ($^1/_4$ pint) stock (see page 45)
1 teaspoon thick cornflour paste (see page 40)

Marinate the beef for at least 2–3 hours. Heat the oil in a preheated wok and fry the steaks for 2 minutes, turning once, remove and drain.

Pour off the excess oil, leaving about 1 tablespoon in the wok, add the ingredients (except the cornflour paste) to make the sauce, bring to the boil and braise the beef steaks in it for about 2 minutes.

Place the steaks on a serving plate, thicken the sauce with the cornflour paste, pour evenly over the beef, garnish with the spring onion and serve hot.

STIR-FRIED LAMB IN SWEET BEAN SAUCE
醬爆羊肉

Serves 4.

Preparation & cooking time: 20–25 mins & marinating time.

A classic dish from Northern China. The spring onions can be substituted by leeks when in season.

275–350g (10–12oz) leg of lamb fillet
10g ($^1/_4$oz) dried black fungus (wood ears, see Glossary)
6–8 spring onions or 225g (8oz) young leeks
about 600ml (1 pint) seasoned oil (see page 44)
a few small bits of fresh ginger root
2 tablespoons yellow bean sauce

For the marinade:
$^1/_4$ teaspoon ground Sichuan red peppercorns
$^1/_2$ teaspoon soft brown sugar
1 tablespoon light soy sauce
2 teaspoons Chinese rice wine
2 teaspoons thick cornflour paste (see page 40)
1 teaspoon sesame oil

Cut the lamb into small thin slices and marinate in the marinade for 2–3 hours – longer if possible.

Soak the wood ears in warm water for 10–15 minutes, rinse, drain, and discard any hard bits. Cut the spring onions or leeks into short strips.

Heat the oil in a preheated wok until hot, blanch the lamb for about 1 minute, stirring to separate the slices; remove as soon as the colour changes, then drain.

Pour off the excess oil, leaving about 1 tablespoon in the wok, add the ginger, spring onions or leeks and wood ears, stir-fry for about 1 minute, then add the yellow bean sauce, blending well, now add the lamb and continue stirring for another minute or so. Serve hot.

STIR-FRIED MIXED VEGETABLES
炒素什錦

Serves 4–6 as a side dish.

Preparation & cooking time: about 25–30 mins.

The ingredients should not be mixed indiscriminately, but carefully selected to achieve a harmonious balance of different colours and contrasting textures.

115g (4oz) Chinese leaves, cut into small pieces
50g (2oz) broccoli spears or mange-tout, topped and tailed
2 small courgettes, thinly sliced diagonally
1 small carrot, thinly sliced diagonally
50–85g (2–3oz) baby corn cobs, halved if large, keep whole if small
50–85g (2–3oz) straw mushrooms, drained and halved (see Glossary)
about 4 tablespoons seasoned oil (see page 44)
1 teaspoon salt
$^1/_2$ teaspoon soft brown sugar
1 tablespoon light soy sauce
pinch of MSG (optional)
a few drops of sesame oil

Prepare the vegetables by cutting them into a roughly uniform shape and size.

Heat the oil in a preheated wok until hot, add the raw vegetables first (canned baby corn cobs and straw mushrooms are pre-cooked, so they only need to be warmed through) and stir-fry for about 2 minutes, then add the canned items with the salt and sugar, continue stirring for another minute, then add the soy sauce and MSG (if using), blend well, garnish with the sesame oil and serve hot or cold.

NB If the vegetables seem too dry in their initial stage of cooking, a little (no more than 2 tablespoons) stock or water can be added to create steam, and also to prevent some of the items getting browned; but remember most vegetables contain quite a lot of water, so you must not have too much 'gravy' for this dish when serving.

BROCCOLI IN OYSTER SAUCE
蠔油西蘭

Serves 4 as a side dish.

Preparation & cooking time: 10–15 mins.

Some Cantonese restaurants use only the stalks of the broccoli for this dish because of their crunchy texture, which is a pity as the spears also have a distinct texture and flavour.

275–350g (10–12oz) broccoli
3–4 tablespoons seasoned oil
a few small bits fresh ginger root
$^1/_4$ teaspoon salt
$^1/_2$ teaspoon soft brown sugar
2 tablespoons stock (see page 45) or water
1–2 tablespoons oyster sauce

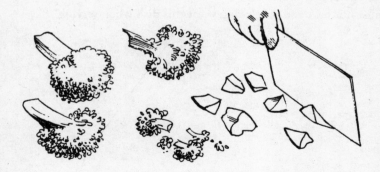

Fig. 24. Preparing the broccoli.

Cut the broccoli spears into small florets; peel off the rough skin from the stalks, and diagonally cut into diamond-shaped chunks.

Heat the oil in a preheated wok until hot, add the bits of ginger and salt (adding salt at this early stage gives the green broccoli an extra bright colour), stir a few times, then add the broccoli, stir-fry for about 2 minutes; now add the sugar and stock or water, blend well and continue stirring for another minute at the most. Pour the oyster sauce over the broccoli, mix and toss once more, then serve hot.

STIR-FRIED LETTUCE HEARTS
蠔油菜芯

Serves 4 as a side dish.

Preparation & cooking time: about 10 mins.

The upright Cos lettuce with its crisp leaves is best for this recipe, or use 2–3 little gems. Alternatively, the hearts of the spring greens used for Crispy 'Seaweed' can be cooked in the same way – only remember to double the cooking time.

1 large Cos lettuce
2–3 tablespoons seasoned oil (see page 44)
3–4 small bits fresh ginger root
a pinch of salt
a pinch of caster sugar
1 tablespoon oyster sauce

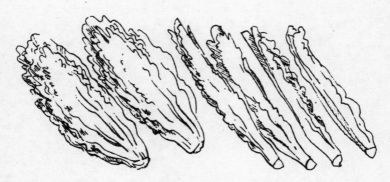

Fig. 25. Preparing the lettuce.

Discard the tough outer leaves of the lettuce, trim off the discoloured root, then cut open lengthways, and, depending on the size of the vegetable, cut into 4–6 long thin strips.

Heat the oil in a preheated wok until hot, add the ginger and salt, stir for a few times before adding the lettuce hearts. Stir-fry for about 1 minute, now adding the sugar and oyster sauce, blend well and serve hot or cold.

STIR-FRIED BEAN SPROUTS
炒芽菜

Serves 4 as a side dish.

Preparation & cooking time: about 10–15 mins.

There is no need to top and tail the sprouts – it is too time-consuming. The most important point to remember here is not to overcook them: that would lose the crispness of texture as well as much of the vitamin C content.

225g (8oz) fresh bean sprouts
3 tablespoons seasoned oil (see page 44)
2–3 spring onions, cut into short sections
$^1/_2$ teaspoon salt
$^1/_2$ teaspoon soft brown sugar
pinch of MSG (optional)

Wash the bean sprouts in cold water and discard any husks and other bits and pieces that float to the surface. Rinse and drain well – get rid of as much excess water as possible.

Heat the oil in a preheated wok until hot, stir-fry the bean sprouts and spring onions together for about 1 minute, then add the salt and sugar, continue stirring for 30–40 seconds more, now add the MSG (if using), blend well and serve hot or cold.

9

IRON-PLATE SIZZLED DISHES

As explained on page 30, iron-plate sizzled dishes are not really authentic Chinese cooking, but they usually create a dramatic appearance at the table in a restaurant.

There are no specific recipes for sizzled dishes – almost any quick stir-fried dishes can be served on a sizzling iron-plate – only remember to reduce the last stage of cooking time by about 30–40 seconds, so that the food will not be over cooked for serving.

Here are just a few recipes specially adapted for iron-plate sizzling. The points to remember, apart from slightly undercooking the food as mentioned above, are that the iron-plate must be preheated to very hot before serving, and that you must keep a distance away from the plate as food is poured onto it, for the hot steam will splutter small beads of oil and gravy all over the place.

Provided that the food is prepared and cooked correctly in the kitchen, you could expect to attain a 98%–100% success rate for any of these dishes.

IRON-PLATE SIZZLED PRAWNS
鐵板蝦

Serves 4.

Preparation & cooking time: 20–25 mins.

This is almost the same recipe as Stir-fried Prawns with Mange-Tout (see page 126), the difference being the Teriyaki sauce in place of soy sauce.

170–225g (6–8oz) uncooked prawns
1 teaspoon salt
$^1/_3$ egg white
2 teaspoons thick cornflour paste (see page 40)
115g (4oz) mange-tout, broccoli, green pepper or any greens
1 small carrot
about 300ml ($^1/_2$ pint) seasoned oil (see page 44)
1 spring onion, cut into short sections
3–4 small bits of fresh ginger root
$^1/_2$ teaspoon soft brown sugar
1 tablespoon Teriyaki sauce
1 teaspoon Chinese rice wine
pinch of MSG (optional)
a few drops of sesame oil

Shell and de-vein the prawns (see page 127), mix with a pinch of salt, the egg white and cornflour paste. Top and tail the mange-tout, or cut the other green vegetables into thin slices. Cut the carrot into thin slices.

Heat the iron-plate before you heat the oil in a preheated wok. Blanch the prawns in the wok for about 30 seconds or until the colour changes, remove and drain.

Pour off the excess oil, leaving about 1 tablespoon in the wok. Add the spring onion, ginger and vegetables, stir-fry for about 1 minute, add the remaining salt and sugar followed by the prawns, stir for a few times, then add the Teriyaki sauce, wine, MSG (if using) and sesame oil, blend well.

To serve: either bring the food on the hot iron-plate sizzling to the table, or put the food on a warm dish and bring it to the table, then pour it into the iron-plate just before serving.

IRON-PLATE SIZZLED CHICKEN
鐵板鷄

Serves 4.

Preparation & cooking time: 20–25 mins.

225g (8oz) chicken breast fillet
1 teaspoon salt
$^1/_3$ egg white
2 teaspoons thick cornflour paste (see page 40)
115g (4oz) mange-tout, broccoli, green pepper or any greens
1 small carrot
about 300ml ($^1/_2$ pint) seasoned oil (see page 44)
1 spring onion, cut into short sections
3–4 small bits of fresh ginger root
$^1/_2$ teaspoon soft brown sugar
1 tablespoon Teriyaki sauce
1 teaspoon Chinese rice wine
pinch of MSG (optional)
a few drops of sesame oil

Cut the chicken into slices about the size of large postage stamps, then mix with a pinch of salt, egg white and cornflour paste.

Top and tail the mange-tout, or cut the other green vegetables into thin slices. Cut the carrot into thin slices.

Heat the iron-plate before you heat the oil in a preheated wok. Blanch the chicken in the wok for about 30 seconds or until the colour changes, remove and drain.

Pour off the excess oil, leaving about 1 tablespoon in the wok. Add the spring onion, ginger and vegetables, stir-fry for about 1 minute, add the remaining salt and sugar followed by the chicken, stir for a few times, then add the Teriyaki sauce, wine, MSG (if using) and sesame oil, blend well.

To serve: either bring the food on the hot iron-plate sizzling to the table, or put the food on a warm dish and bring it to the table, then pour it into the iron-plate just before serving.

IRON-PLATE SIZZLED BEEF
鐵板牛肉

Serves 4.

Preparation & cooking: 20–25 mins & marinating.

275g (10oz) beef steak, such as topside rump
115g (4oz) mange-tout, broccoli, green pepper or any greens
1 small carrot
4–6 small dried Chinese mushrooms, soaked (see Glossary)
about 300ml ($^1/_2$ pint) seasoned oil (see page 44)
1 spring onion, cut into short sections
3–4 small bits of fresh ginger root
$^1/_2$ teaspoon salt
$^1/_2$ teaspoon soft brown sugar
2 tablespoons oyster sauce

For the marinade:
$^1/_4$ teaspoon soft brown sugar
$^1/_2$ tablespoon light soy sauce
1 teaspoon Chinese rice wine
$^1/_3$ teaspoon bicarbonate of soda or baking powder
2 teaspoons thick cornflour paste (see page 40)
2 teaspoons oil

Cut the beef across the grain into slices about the size of large postage stamps, then marinate in the marinade for several hours – the longer the better.

Top and tail the mange-tout, or cut the other green vegetables into thin slices. Cut the carrot into thin slices. Squeeze dry the mushrooms and discard any hard stalks.

Heat the iron-plate before you heat the oil in a preheated wok. Blanch the beef in the wok for about 30–40 seconds or until the colour changes, remove and drain.

Pour off the excess oil, leaving about 1 tablespoon in the wok. Add the spring onion, ginger and vegetables, stir-fry for about 1 minute, add the salt and sugar followed by the beef, stir for a few times, then add the oyster sauce, blending well.

To serve: either bring the food on the hot iron-plate sizzling to the table, or put the food on a warm dish and bring it to the table, then pour it into the iron-plate just before serving.

IRON-PLATE SIZZLED LAMB
鐵板羊肉

Serves 4.

Preparation & cooking time: 20–25 mins & marinating time.

350g (12oz) leg of lamb fillet
about 600ml (1 pint) seasoned oil (see page 44)
6–8 spring onions, cut into short sections
3–4 small bits of fresh ginger root
1 tablespoon yellow bean sauce
1 tablespoon Worcester sauce

For the marinade:
$1/4$ teaspoon soft brown sugar
pinch of ground white pepper
1 tablespoon Teriyaki sauce
1 teaspoon Chinese rice wine
2 teaspoons thick cornflour paste (see page 40)
2 teaspoons sesame oil

Cut the lamb across the grain into slices about the size of large postage stamps, then marinate in the marinade for several hours – the longer the better.

Heat the iron-plate before you heat the oil in a preheated wok. Blanch the lamb in the wok for about 30–40 seconds or until the colour changes, remove and drain.

Pour off the excess oil, leaving about 1 tablespoon in the wok. Add the spring onion and ginger, stir-fry for about 30 seconds, then add the crushed yellow bean sauce, blend well, now add the lamb, stir for a few times, then add the Worcester sauce, again blending well.

To serve: either bring the food on the hot iron-plate sizzling to the table, or put the food on a warm dish and bring it to the table, then pour it into the iron-plate just before serving.

IRON-PLATE SIZZLED SEAFOOD
鐵板海鮮

Serves 4.

Preparation & cooking time: 30–35 mins.

115g (4oz) cleaned squid
115g (4oz) uncooked prawns
3–4 fresh scallops
$1/4$ egg white
2 teaspoons thick cornflour paste (see page 40)
115g (4oz) mange-tout, broccoli, green pepper or any greens
1 small carrot
about 300ml ($1/2$ pint) seasoned oil (see page 44)
1 spring onion, cut into short sections
3–4 small bits of fresh ginger root
$1/2$ teaspoon salt
$1/2$ teaspoon soft brown sugar
1 tablespoon Teriyaki sauce
1 teaspoon Chinese rice wine
a few drops of sesame oil

Prepare and blanch the squid as for Deep-Fried Squid on page 82. Shell and de-vein the prawns (see page 127), then cut each one in half lengthways. Cut each scallop into 3–4 slices. Mix the prawns and scallops with the egg white and cornflour paste.

Top and tail the mange-tout, or cut the other green vegetables into thin slices. Cut the carrot into thin slices.

Heat the iron-plate before you heat the oil in a preheated wok. Blanch the seafood in the wok for about 30 seconds, remove and drain.

Pour off the excess oil, leaving about 1 tablespoon in the wok. Add the spring onion, ginger, and vegetables, stir-fry for about 1 minute, add the salt and sugar followed by the seafood, stir for a few times, then add the Teriyaki sauce, wine and sesame oil, blending well.

To serve: either bring the food on the hot iron-plate sizzling to the table, or put the food on a warm dish and bring it to the table, then pour it into the iron-plate just before serving.

10
BRAISED DISHES

Most dishes in this section are served as the main course since they all contain a certain amount of sauce or gravy. Basically, there are two types of braising:

Quick Braising: this is one of the most used cooking techniques in Chinese cooking. It is very similar to stir-frying; the only difference in quick braising is that the ingredients are cut into small pieces and deep-fried first, then a sauce is made and the food is 'stir-braised' in the sauce for a very short time – usually less than a minute.

Long Braising: sometimes known as 'red cooking', this method is rather like 'stewing'. The ingredients are first cut into small chunks, then fried, deep-fried, par boiled or steamed until half-cooked; seasonings (soy sauce, wine, ginger and sugar, etc) and stock or water are then added to them, then the mixture is brought to the boil and simmered for a long time (anything from 10 minutes to over an hour).

High marks are possible for all these dishes, particularly for long braising dishes – say a 95%–100% success rate. Good luck!

DUCK WITH PINEAPPLE
菠蘿鴨絲

Serves 4.

Preparation & cooking time: 20–25 mins.

You will need ready-cooked duck meat for this dish – so use any leftovers from Soy-braised Duck (see page 54), Roast Duck – Cantonese Style (see page 102), or Peking Duck (see page 104).

115–175g (4–6oz) ready-cooked duck meat
3 tablespoons seasoned oil (see page 44)
1 small onion, thinly sliced
a few small bits of fresh ginger root
1 spring onion, cut into short sections
1 small carrot, thinly shredded
about 115g (4oz) pineapple rings, drained and cut into small slices
$1/2$ teaspoon salt
1 tablespoon rice vinegar
2–3 tablespoons syrup from the pineapple
1 teaspoon thin cornflour paste (see page 40)

Cut the duck meat into fine shreds.

Heat the oil in a preheated wok, stir-fry the onion until opaque, then add the ginger, spring onion and carrot; stir-fry for about 2 minutes, then add the duck and pineapple with the seasonings and syrup, blend well and bring to the boil; thicken the sauce with the cornflour paste and serve.

SWEET AND SOUR PRAWNS
甜酸明蝦

Serves 4.

Preparation & cooking time: 25–30 mins.

There are several different versions of this highly popular dish. Obviously the most important item is the sauce – not too much tomato ketchup should be used.

175–225g (6–8oz) uncooked tiger prawns
pinch of salt
$1/4$ egg white
1 teaspoon thick cornflour paste (see page 40)
about 300ml ($1/2$ pint) seasoned oil (see page 44)

For the sauce:
1 tablespoon seasoned oil (see page 44)
$1/2$ small onion, cut into small thin slices
$1/2$ small carrot, thinly sliced diagonally
about 115g (4oz) water chestnuts, drained and sliced
2 tablespoons soft brown sugar
3 tablespoons rice vinegar
1 tablespoon light soy sauce
1 teaspoon Chinese rice wine
1 teaspoon tomato sauce (ketchup or purée, as you prefer)
about 4 tablespoons stock (see page 45) or water
2 teaspoons thin cornflour paste (see page 40)
a few drops of sesame oil

Shell and de-vein the prawns (see page 127), mix with the salt, egg white and thick cornflour paste. Heat the oil in a preheated wok and deep-fry the prawns in warm oil for about 30–40 seconds, remove and drain.

Wipe the wok clean, heat the tablespoon of fresh oil, stir-fry the onion, carrot and water chestnuts for about 1 minute, now add the sugar, vinegar, soy sauce, wine, tomato sauce and stock or water, bring to the boil, then add the prawns, blend well and braise for 30–40 seconds, stirring constantly; finally thicken the sauce with the thin cornflour paste, add the sesame oil and serve.

SWEET AND SOUR FISH
甜酸魚片

Serves 4.

Preparation & cooking: 25–30 mins & marinating.

For best result, use firm white fish fillet from the tail end.

350–400g (12–14 oz) fish fillet (cod, haddock or plaice, etc)
1 tablespoon light soy sauce
1 teaspoon Chinese rice wine or brandy
1 egg, beaten
3 tablespoons plain flour mixed with 1 tablespoon water
oil for deep-frying

For the sauce:
1 tablespoon seasoned oil (see page 44)
$^1/_2$ small onion, cut into small thin slices
$^1/_2$ small carrot, thinly sliced diagonally
$^1/_4$ cucumber, halved lengthwise, then sliced diagonally
$^1/_2$ teaspoon finely chopped garlic
1 tablespoon light soy sauce
2 tablespoons soft brown sugar
3 tablespoons rice vinegar
1 tablespoon tomato sauce (ketchup or purée)
about 4 tablespoons stock (see page 45) or water
2 teaspoons thin cornflour paste (see page 40)
a few drops of sesame oil

Dry the fish well, then cut it into matchbox-size pieces and marinate in the soy sauce and wine for 10–15 minutes. Make a batter with the egg and flour.

Coat the fish pieces with the batter. Deep-fry them in hot oil for 2–3 minutes or until golden brown, remove and drain.

Wipe the wok clean, heat the tablespoon of fresh oil until hot, stir-fry the vegetables with the garlic for about 1 minute, now add the soy sauce, sugar, vinegar, tomato sauce and stock or water, bring to the boil, then add the fish, blending well; thicken the sauce with the cornflour paste, garnish with the sesame oil, and toss a few times off the heat. Serve hot.

BRAISED FISH FILLET IN WINE SAUCE
糟溜魚片

Serves 4.

Preparation & cooking time: 25–30 mins.

450g (1lb) lemon sole or plaice fillet
pinch of salt
$^1/_2$ egg white, lightly beaten
1 tablespoon thick cornflour paste (see page 40)
oil for deep-frying

For the sauce:
10g ($^1/_4$oz) dried black fungus (wood ears, see Glossary)
1 tablespoon seasoned oil (see page 44)
$^1/_2$ teaspoon finely chopped garlic
1 teaspoon salt
2 teaspoons soft brown sugar
2 tablespoons Chinese rice wine or dry sherry
1 tablespoon brandy, whisky or rum
about 100ml (4fl oz) stock (see page 45) or water
a pinch of MSG (optional)
a few drops of sesame oil
2 teaspoons thin cornflour paste (see page 40)

Trim off the soft bones along the edges of the fish. Cut each fillet into 8–10 pieces if large, or 4–6 pieces if small. Mix with the salt, egg white and thick cornflour paste, blend gently with fingers.

Soak the wood ears in warm water for 10–15 minutes, rinse and drain, cut into small pieces.

Heat the oil until medium hot, add the fish piece by piece, and stir gently to make sure they are not stuck together. Deep-fry for about 1 minute, remove and drain.

Wipe clean the wok, heat the tablespoon of fresh oil until hot, stir-fry the wood ears with the garlic for 30–40 seconds, add the salt, sugar, wine, brandy and stock or water, bring to the boil, then add the fish, blend well and braise for about 1 minute. Now add the MSG (if using) and sesame oil, and thicken the sauce with the thin cornflour paste off the heat. Serve hot.

BRAISED WHOLE FISH
紅燒魚

Serves 4-6.

Preparation & cooking time: 20–25 mins & marinating time.

This is a basic recipe – a whole fish is first deep-fried, then braised in a specially prepared sauce such as 'Spring onion and ginger', 'Chilli and garlic', etc.

1 whole fish (sea bass, bream, trout, grouper or grey mullet, etc)
    weighing about 675g (1¹/₂lb), cleaned
1 tablespoon light soy sauce
1 tablespoon Chinese rice wine
oil for deep-frying
fresh coriander leaves to garnish

For the sauce:
1 tablespoon thinly shredded fresh ginger root
2–3 spring onions, thinly shredded
2 tablespoons yellow bean sauce
about 100ml (4fl oz) stock (see page 45) or water
a few drops of sesame oil

Make sure the fish is scaled and gutted. Wash and dry well on kitchen paper. Score both sides of the fish diagonally as far as the bone at intervals of about 2.5cm (1"). Marinate in the soy sauce and wine for 10–15 minutes.

Deep-fry the fish in hot oil for about 3–4 minutes, turning once. Pour off the excess oil, leaving about 1 tablespoon in the wok. Push the fish to one side of the wok and add the ingredients for the sauce (except the sesame oil), bring to the boil, and braise the fish in it for 4–5 minutes, turning once.

Finally, add the sesame oil and serve, garnished with coriander leaves.

NB For a 'hot and spicy' version, add 1 teaspoon finely chopped garlic (and finely chop the ginger and spring onions), and instead of yellow bean sauce, use 1 tablespoon chilli bean sauce (see Glossary); also add a little sugar and rice vinegar as well as a little tomato purée or ketchup (whichever you prefer). The cooking method is exactly the same.

LOBSTER WITH BLACK BEANS
豉椒焗龍蝦

Serves 4–6.

Preparation & cooking time: about 25–30 mins.

Only live lobsters are used in Chinese restaurants as ready-cooked ones have been boiled for far too long, thereby losing much of their delicate flavour and texture.

1 large or 2 medium lobsters
oil for deep-frying
fresh coriander leaves to garnish

For the sauce:
1 teaspoon finely chopped garlic
1 teaspoon finely chopped fresh ginger root
2–3 spring onions, cut into short sections
2 tablespoons black bean sauce
1 tablespoon Chinese rice wine
about 100ml (4fl oz) stock (see page 45) or water

Cut the lobster in half lengthways (starting from the head). Discard the legs, intestines, and the feathery lungs. Remove the claws and crack them with the back of the cleaver.

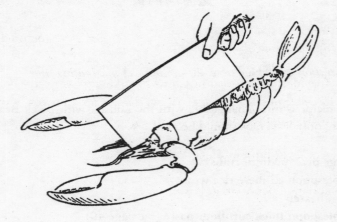

Fig. 26. Cutting the lobster.

Deep-fry the lobster pieces in hot oil for about 2–3 minutes, or until the colour turns bright orange. Remove and drain.

Pour off the excess oil, leaving about 1 tablespoon in the wok, add the garlic, ginger, spring onions and black bean sauce, stir-fry for a few seconds, then add the wine and stock, bring to the boil; now add the lobster pieces, blend well and braise for about 2–3 minutes under cover. Serve garnished with the coriander leaves.

NB Both this lobster and the following crab dish should be served with finger bowls and plenty of paper tissues, as they are best eaten with fingers!

CRAB WITH SPRING ONIONS
AND GINGER
薑葱焗肉蟹

Serves 4–6.

Preparation & cooking time: 20–25 mins & marinating time.

This recipe is inter-changeable with the Lobster with Black Beans.
Again, only live crabs should be used.

1 large or 2 medium crabs
1 tablespoon Chinese rice wine
1 egg, beaten
1 tablespoon thick cornflour paste (see page 40)
3–4 tablespoons seasoned oil (see page 44)
1 tablespoon finely chopped fresh ginger root
3–4 spring onions, cut into short sections
2 tablespoons light soy sauce
1 teaspoon soft brown sugar
about 100ml (4fl oz) stock (see page 45) or water
a few drops of sesame oil

Cut the crab in half from the under-belly. Open the shell and discard
the feathery gills and the sac shown alongside the main drawing in
fig. 27. Break off the claws and legs, crack the shells of the claws and
legs with the back of the cleaver; cut the body into several pieces.
Marinate the claws, legs and all the crab pieces with the wine, egg
and cornflour paste for 10–15 minutes.

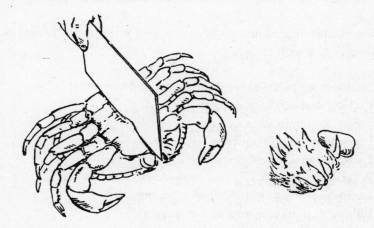

Fig 27. Preparing the crab.

Heat the oil in a preheated wok and stir-fry the crab pieces with
the ginger and spring onions for 2–3 minutes, now add the soy
sauce, sugar and stock or water, blend well and bring to the boil;
braise for 4–5 minutes, stirring constantly. Garnish with the sesame
oil and serve hot as per page 187.

CHILLI CHICKEN – SICHUAN STYLE
辣子鷄

Serves 4.

Preparation & cooking time: 25–30 mins & marinating time.

Use chicken legs (thighs and drumsticks) for this dish – breasts are best for quick stir-frying.

2 chicken leg portions (or 2 thighs and 2 drumsticks)
1 tablespoon soft brown sugar
2 teaspoons light soy sauce
1 teaspoon dark soy sauce
1 tablespoon Chinese rice wine
$1/4$ teaspoon crushed Sichuan peppercorns
2 teaspoons thick cornflour paste (see page 40)
300ml ($1/2$ pint) seasoned oil (see page 44)
2 cloves garlic, crushed
2–3 spring onions, cut into short sections with white and green
    parts separated
4–6 small dried red chillies, seeded and cut into small bits
2 tablespoons yellow bean sauce
about 150ml ($1/4$ pint) stock (see page 45) or water

Chop the chicken through the bone into small bite-sized pieces. Marinate in the sugar, soy sauces, wine, pepper and cornflour paste for at least 25–30 minutes – the longer, the better.

Heat the oil to hot and deep-fry the chicken pieces for 1–2 minutes only, remove and drain.

Pour off excess oil, leaving about 1 teaspoon in the wok, add the garlic, spring onions (white parts only at this stage), chillies and yellow bean sauce, stir-fry for about 15–20 seconds, then add the chicken pieces, blend well and add the stock or water, and bring to the boil. Braise for 5–6 minutes over medium heat under cover, stirring once or twice. Now add the green parts of the spring onions, turn the heat to high and braise (this time uncovered) for another minute or so until the sauce is entirely absorbed. Serve hot.

BRAISED CHICKEN WINGS
蜜汁鷄翼

Serves 4–6.

Preparation & cooking time: 20–25 mins & marinating time.

The sweetness of the honey contrasts well with the soy-braised chicken wings.

12 chicken wings, without the pinions
2 teaspoons soft brown sugar
2 teaspoons dark soy sauce
1 tablespoon light soy sauce
1 tablespoon Chinese rice wine
about 300ml ($^1/_2$ pint) seasoned oil (see page 44)
$^1/_2$ teaspoon finely chopped fresh ginger root
1 tablespoon finely chopped spring onions
2 tablespoons yellow bean sauce
150ml (about 5fl oz) stock (see page 45) or water
1 tablespoon honey

Marinate the chicken wings in the sugar, soy sauces and wine for at least 1 hour – longer if possible.

Heat the oil until hot and deep-fry the chicken wings for about 2–3 minutes, or until golden brown; remove and drain.

Pour off the excess oil, leaving about 1 teaspoon in the wok, add the ginger, spring onions and yellow bean sauce, stir-fry for about 30–40 seconds, then add the chicken wings with the marinade, and blend well. Now add the stock or water, bring to the boil, reduce the heat and braise for 8–10 minutes under cover, stirring once or twice.

Now remove the cover, turn the heat to high again, and reduce the sauce until it is 'sticky' and rich; add the honey and blend well. Serve hot.

CHICKEN FU-YUNG
芙蓉鷄

Serves 4.

Preparation & cooking time: about 25–30 mins.

In most Chinese restaurants, a 'fu-yung' dish usually means omelette or scrambled eggs, but strictly speaking, *fu-yung* in Chinese means 'lotus-white' which should be creamy-textured egg whites that have been lightly deep-fried. This prompted some imaginative cooks to call this dish 'Deep-fried Milk'!

Use the best part of the breastmeat for this recipe i.e. the strip just along the breastbone – known as 'chicken goujon' or 'inner fillet'.

115–175g (4–6 oz) chicken breastmeat
pinch of salt
4 egg whites, lightly beaten
1 tablespoon thick cornflour paste (see page 40)
2 tablespoons milk
about 600ml (1 pint) oil for deep-frying
about 100ml (4fl oz) stock (see page 45)
1 tablespoon peas
2 teaspoons Chinese rice wine
a pinch of MSG (optional)
a few drops of sesame oil
1 teaspoon finely minced ham to garnish

Finely mince the chicken meat, mix with the salt, egg white, cornflour paste and milk; blend well.

Heat the oil in a very hot wok. Pour the chicken and egg white mixture into the wok in batches – do not stir this mixture, otherwise it will scatter, but gently stir the oil from the bottom of the wok so that the 'fu-yung' will rise to the surface. Remove as soon as the colour turns bright white; drain.

Wipe the wok clean, bring the stock to the boil, add the peas, chicken and wine, bring to the boil, then add the MSG (if using) and sesame oil, blend well. Serve garnished with the ham.

NB Prawns or crabmeat can be substituted for the chicken.

BRAISED PORK SPARE-RIBS
豉椒排骨

Serves 4.

Preparation & cooking time: 25–30 mins & marinating time.

You definitely need a Chinese cleaver to chop the spare-ribs into
bite-size pieces for this dish.

450–550g (1–1¹/₄lb) pork spare-ribs
1 tablespoon soft brown sugar
1 teaspoon dark soy sauce
2 teaspoons light soy sauce
1 tablespoon Chinese rice wine
2 teaspoons cornflour
about 600ml (1 pint) seasoned oil (see page 44)
1 teaspoon chopped garlic
2–3 spring onions, cut into short sections
1–2 small hot green or red chillies, cut into small bits*
2 tablespoons black bean sauce
about 150ml (¹/₄ pint) stock (see page 45) or water
1 medium green pepper, seeded and cored, cut into small cubes

Remove excess fat, then chop each individual rib into 3–4 bite-size pieces, then marinate in the sugar, soy sauces, wine and cornflour for at least 1 hour.

Heat the oil until hot, deep-fry the ribs for about 1–2 minutes or until golden brown, remove and drain.

Pour off the excess oil, leaving about 2 teaspoons in the wok, stir-fry the garlic, spring onions, chillies and black bean sauce for about 30–40 seconds, add the spare-ribs, and blend well; now add the stock or water with the marinade, bring to the boil, reduce the heat and braise under cover for 8–10 minutes, stirring once or twice and adding a little more stock or water if necessary. Finally, uncover and add the green pepper, increase the heat to high again, and stir-braise for 1 more minute to reduce the sauce. Serve hot.

*NB Handle fresh chillies with great care. See page 52.

BRAISED BRISKET OF BEEF
紅燒牛腩

Serves 5–6.

Preparation & cooking time: 2¹/₄ hours.

675g (1¹/₂lb) brisket of beef (or shin, shank)
about 600ml (1 pint) boiling water
1 tablespoon soft brown sugar
2 tablespoons seasoned oil (see page 44)
1 teaspoon finely chopped fresh ginger root
1 tablespoon finely chopped spring onions
3 tablespoons light soy sauce
1 tablespoon dark soy sauce
2 tablespoons Chinese rice wine or brandy
25g (1oz) rock candy or crystal sugar
1 teaspoon five-spice powder
2–3 teaspoons thin cornflour paste (see page 40)

Trim the beef of excess fat, cut into matchbox-size chunks. Blanch in a pan of boiling water for 3 minutes, then turn off the heat and remove the beef with a strainer.

Add the sugar to the liquid. After 10 minutes or so, all the impurities will sink to the bottom of the pan, leaving the 'stock' clear. Drain it through a fine sieve and reserve.

Heat the oil in a preheated wok or pan, stir-fry the ginger and spring onions for a few seconds, then add the beef and stir-fry for 2–3 minutes. Now add the soy sauces and wine, blend well, then add the rock sugar and five-spice powder with about half of the reserved 'stock', bring to the boil, reduce the heat and braise under cover for about 2 hours.

Check the level of the liquid now and again – it should just cover the meat – top it up with more liquid if it seems to be too dry. Finally, uncover and thicken the gravy with the cornflour paste. Serve hot.

NB Any other cheap cuts of meat such as neck or breast of lamb, stewing veal and belly pork, etc, can all be cooked by the same method. But you may need to reduce the cooking time for the very last stage slightly – say by 20–30 minutes or so.

BRAISED BEAN-CURD HOME STYLE
家常豆腐

Serves 4.

Preparation & cooking time: 20–25 mins & soaking time for mushrooms.

Bean-curd (*tofu*) is widely used in everyday home cooking in China. It has a rather unusual texture, and is an acquired taste. It is exceptionally high in protein and is most useful in absorbing and harmonizing the flavour of other ingredients.

4–5 small dried Chinese mushrooms (see Glossary)
85–115g (3–4oz) lean pork
2 cakes bean-curd
about 600ml (1 pint) seasoned oil (see page 44)
2 spring onions, cut into short sections
3–4 small dried whole red chillies, soaked (optional)
1 tablespoon light soy sauce
2 tablespoons yellow bean sauce
1 tablespoon Chinese rice wine
about 3–4 tablespoons stock (see page 45) or water
a pinch of MSG (optional)
a few drops of sesame oil

Soak the mushrooms in cold water for 50–60 minutes, squeeze dry and discard any hard stalks, thinly shred the remainder. Cut the pork into thin shreds too. Split each cake of bean-curd crossways into 3–4 slices, then cut each slice diagonally into 2 triangles.

Heat the oil until hot, deep-fry the bean-curd pieces for 2–3 minutes, or until both sides are golden. Remove and drain.

Pour off excess oil, leaving about 1 tablespoon in the wok, stir-fry the spring onions and red chillies (if using) with the pork and mushrooms for about 1 minute, then add the bean-curd with the soy sauce, yellow bean sauce and wine, blending well. Now add the stock or water, bring to the boil and stir-braise for 2 minutes. Finally, add the MSG (if using) and sesame oil, blend well and serve hot.

MA-PO TOFU
(BEAN-CURD SICHUAN STYLE)
麻婆豆腐

Serves 4.

Preparation & cooking time: 20–25mins.

Ma-Po was the wife of a Sichuan chef who worked in the provincial capital Chengdu in the 19th century. This universally popular dish has a number of variations – some restaurants list it as 'Spicy bean-curd' or just simply as 'Sichuan bean-curd'.

2–3 cakes bean-curd
3 tablespoons seasoned oil (see page 44)
115g (4oz) beef, coarsely chopped
1 leek or 2–3 spring onions, cut into short sections
1 teaspoon chopped garlic
1 tablespoon black bean sauce
1 tablespoon light soy sauce
1 teaspoon chilli bean sauce
1 tablespoon Chinese rice wine
about 3–4 tablespoons stock (see page 45)
$^1/_2$ teaspoon ground Sichuan red peppercorns
pinch of MSG (optional)
2 teaspoons thin cornflour paste (see page 40)
a few drops of sesame oil

Cut the bean-curd into 1cm (½") square cubes; blanch in a pan of boiling water for 2–3 minutes to harden. Remove and drain.

Heat the oil in a preheated wok, stir-fry the beef for about 1 minute or until the colour changes, now add the leek or spring onions, garlic and black bean sauce, stir-fry for another minute, then add the bean-curd, soy sauce, chilli bean sauce and wine; blend well and add the stock, bring to the boil and braise for another minute. Finally add the Sichuan pepper and MSG (if using), thicken the sauce with the cornflour paste and garnish with the sesame oil. Serve hot.

'FISH-FLAVOURED' (YU-HSIANG) AUBERGINE
魚香茄子

Serves 4.

Preparation & cooking time: 20–25 mins.

Yu-Hsiang, which literally means 'fish fragrance', is a Sichuan cookery term indicating that the dish is cooked with seasonings originally used for a fish recipe.

450g (1lb) aubergines
600ml (1 pint) oil
85–115g (3–4oz) lean pork, thinly shredded
$^1/_2$ teaspoon chopped garlic
$^1/_2$ teaspoon finely chopped fresh ginger root
1 teaspoon finely chopped white section of spring onions
3–4 small dried red chillies, soaked and cut into small bits
1 teaspoon soft brown sugar
1 tablespoon light soy sauce
2 teaspoons chilli bean sauce
1 tablespoon Chinese rice wine
1 tablespoon rice vinegar
2 teaspoons thin cornflour paste (see page 40)
pinch of MSG (optional)
2 teaspoons finely chopped green spring onions
a few drops of sesame oil

Cut the aubergines into short strips the size of potato chips (the skin can either be peeled or be left on as you prefer). Deep-fry them in hot oil for 3–4 minutes or until limp. Remove and drain.

Pour off the excess oil, leaving about 1 tablespoon in the wok, stir-fry the pork shreds with the garlic, ginger, spring onion whites and chillies for about 1 minute, now add the sugar, soy sauce, chilli bean sauce, wine and vinegar followed by the aubergines, blend well and braise for another minute. Finally thicken the sauce with the cornflour paste, add the MSG (if using), green spring onions and sesame oil. Serve hot.

BRAISED CHINESE MUSHROOMS AND BAMBOO SHOOTS

炒雙冬

Serves 4.

Preparation & cooking time: 10–15 mins & soaking time for mushrooms.

The Chinese name for this dish is 'The Twin Winters', because both mushrooms and bamboo shoots are at their best during the winter season. Therefore you should really use 'Winter Bamboo Shoots' and 'extra fat' mushrooms.

50g (2oz) dried Chinese mushrooms (see Glossary)
225–275g (8–10oz) winter bamboo shoots
3 tablespoons seasoned oil (see page 44)
1–2 spring onions, cut into short sections
2 tablespoons light soy sauce or oyster sauce
1 tablespoon Chinese rice wine
½ teaspoon soft brown sugar
2 teaspoons thin cornflour paste
a few drops of sesame oil

Soak the mushrooms in *warm* water for at least 1 hour, squeeze dry and discard any hard stalks (but reserve the water). Cut them in half or quarter if large, leave whole if small.

Drain and rinse the bamboo shoots, cut them into small wedge-shape chunks.

Heat the oil in a preheated wok, add the spring onions and stir-fry with the mushrooms and bamboo shoots for about 1 minute, add the soy sauce or oyster sauce, wine and sugar with about 2–3 tablespoons of the mushroom-soaking water, blend well and bring to the boil; braise for another minute or so, then thicken the gravy with the cornflour paste. Garnish with the sesame oil and serve.

CHICKEN/MEAT CURRY
咖喱鷄／肉

Serves 4.

Preparation & cooking time: about 1¹/₂ hours.

Curry dishes from a Chinese restaurant are quite different from those served in an Indian establishment – what you need is to get the special curry powder mixture from a Chinese supermarket.

450g (1lb) chicken, beef, or lamb, etc. cut into small cubes
1 teaspoon soft brown sugar
1 tablespoon light soy sauce
1 tablespoon Chinese rice wine
1 tablespoon cornflour
3 tablespoons seasoned oil (see page 44)
¹/₂ teaspoon chopped garlic
1 medium onion, finely chopped
2 tablespoons mild curry powder
stock (see page 45) or water
1 teaspoon salt
1 tablespoon dark soy sauce
1–2 teaspoons chilli sauce (optional)

Marinate the chicken/meat pieces in the sugar, light soy sauce, wine and cornflour for 25–30 minutes.

Heat the oil in a wok or pot, lightly brown the garlic and onion over low heat, add the curry powder, mix and allow it to brown, then add a little stock or water to make a smooth paste by stirring constantly. Now add the chicken/meat pieces and cook on a high heat for about 5 minutes, again stirring constantly to prevent it from sticking to the bottom of the pan. Add the salt, dark soy sauce and just enough stock or water to cover; reduce the heat and braise under cover until tender – chicken requires only 25–30 minutes cooking time, pork and lamb need 45–50 minutes, but beef will take 60–65 minutes. Finally add the chilli sauce (if using), blend well and serve.

11

CASSEROLES

As mentioned on page 29 in Essential Equipment, the traditional Chinese casserole is an earthenware pot, known as a Sand-Pot or Clay-Pot.

Casseroles are among the most ancient cooking utensils. It is speculated that the first earthenware pot evolved from the technique of cooking fowl or small animals by encasing them in mud or wet clay, then baking them in hot stones and ashes. By the time the food was cooked, the mud or clay had hardened, and the art of pottery was born.

Chinese casseroles are meant for stove-top cooking. Because they are unglazed on the outside, they are porous and have to be 'seasoned' before placing directly over gas or electric heat for the very first time.

There are two ways of doing this: Either soak the casserole in water for 24 hours, then dry thoroughly before use. Or rub the outside bottom surface with a cut clove of garlic until the entire surface is darkened and moist, then fill the pot with salted water, place it over a low heat and slowly bring the water to the boil; let it boil for 4–5 minutes, remove the pot from the heat and leave to cool before emptying the water, and drying the pot thoroughly.

Two important points to remember: *never* place an empty sand-pot on the heat – there should always be liquid (water or oil) in the pot to prevent it from cracking. *Never* place a hot casserole on a damp or cold surface – the combination of hot pot and wet or cold surface will crack the pot.

Apart from that, casserole cooking is easy and simple, therefore you should achieve a success rating of 95–100% for all the dishes.

FISH AND BEAN-CURD CASSEROLE
魚球豆腐煲

Serves 4–6.

Preparation & cooking time: about 35–40 mins.

This dish is light and delicious – low in calories, high in protein.

450g (1lb) firm white fish steak (cod, haddock or monkfish)
1 egg, beaten
2 tablespoons plain flour mixed with 1 tablespoon water
4–5 small dried Chinese mushrooms, soaked (see Glossary)
2 cakes bean-curd
oil for deep-frying
a few lettuce or Chinese leaves
about 300ml ($^1/_2$ pint) stock (see page 45) or water
1 teaspoon salt
1 teaspoon soft brown sugar
1 tablespoon light soy sauce
1 tablespoon Chinese rice wine
4–5 small bits fresh ginger root
2 spring onions, cut into short sections
fresh coriander leaves to garnish

Cut each fish steak into several small chunks. Coat each piece with egg and flour.

Squeeze dry the mushrooms, discard any hard stalks. Cut them in half if large, leave them whole if small. Cut each cake of bean-curd into 16 pieces.

Heat the oil in a wok or deep-fryer and fry the bean-curd pieces for 3–4 minutes or until golden, remove and drain. Deep-fry the fish pieces in the same oil for 3–4 minutes or until golden, remove and drain.

Line a casserole with the lettuce or Chinese leaves, add about 3–4 tablespoons stock or water. Place the bean-curd and fish pieces in the casserole, add the mushrooms, seasonings and the remaining stock, bring to the boil over a high heat, then reduce the heat and braise under cover for 10–15 minutes. Serve hot, garnished with sprigs of coriander leaves.

SEAFOOD CASSEROLE
海鮮豆腐保

Serves 4–6.

Preparation & cooking time: 30–35 mins.

This is the Chinese version of the French *bouillabaisse* in which several different kinds of fish and shellfish are cooked together with vegetables.

450g (1lb) assorted fish steaks or fillet, such as cod, haddock, monkfish, whiting, salmon or eel, etc
1 teaspoon salt
1 egg white
1 tablespoon thick cornflour paste (see page 40)
225g (8oz) assorted shellfish (prawns, scallops, mussels, oysters or whelks, etc)
4–5 small dried Chinese mushrooms, soaked (see Glossary)
2 cakes bean-curd
oil for deep-frying
a few lettuce or Chinese leaves
about 300ml (¹/₂ pint) stock (see page 45) or water
50g (2oz) lean pork, thinly shredded
1 teaspoon soft brown sugar
2 tablespoons light soy sauce
2 tablespoons Chinese rice wine
4–5 small bits fresh ginger root
2 spring onions, cut into short sections
fresh coriander leaves to garnish

Cut the fish into several small chunks, mix with the salt, egg white and cornflour paste. Shell or peel the shellfish as necessary.

Squeeze dry the mushrooms, discard any hard stalks and thinly shred. Cut each cake of bean-curd into 16 pieces.

Heat the oil in a wok or deep-fryer and fry the bean-curd pieces for 3–4 minutes or until golden, remove and drain. Deep-fry the fish pieces in the same oil for 3–4 minutes or until golden, remove and drain.

Line a casserole with the lettuce or Chinese leaves, add about 3–4 tablespoons stock or water. Place the bean-curd and fish pieces in the casserole, add the shellfish, mushrooms, pork, seasonings and the remaining stock, bring to the boil over a high heat, then reduce the heat and braise under cover for 10–15 minutes. Serve hot, garnished with sprigs of coriander leaves.

MIXED MEAT CASSEROLE
什錦砂鍋

Serves 4–6.

Preparation & cooking time: 25–30 mins.

The Chinese often make harmonious combinations of different ingredients in one single dish and give it a poetic descriptive name. Alternative names for this recipe are 'Eight-Treasure' or 'Precious'. But it is not necessary to have eight different ingredients for this dish – the number eight just sounds good.

4–5 small dried Chinese mushrooms, soaked (see Glossary)
2 cakes bean-curd
oil for deep-frying
a few lettuce or Chinese leaves
about 300ml ($^1/_2$ pint) stock (see page 45) or water
450g (1lb) assorted cooked meats such as Char Siu, (see page 100), Roasted Crispy Pork, (see page 97), Roast Duck (see page 102), Crispy-Skin Chicken (see page 96) or White-Cut Chicken (see page 50), etc
225g (8oz) assorted shellfish (prawns, scallops, etc)
1 teaspoon soft brown sugar
1 tablespoon oyster sauce
1 tablespoon Chinese rice wine
4–5 small bits fresh ginger root
2 spring onions, cut into short sections

Squeeze dry the mushrooms, discard any hard stalks and thinly shred. Cut each cake of bean-curd into 16 pieces.

Heat the oil in a wok or deep-fryer and fry the bean-curd pieces for 3–4 minutes or until golden, remove and drain.

Line a casserole with the lettuce or Chinese leaves, add about 3–4 tablespoons stock or water. Place the bean-curd and meat pieces in the casserole, add the mushrooms, shellfish, seasonings and the remaining stock, bring to the boil over a high heat, then reduce the heat and braise under cover for 10–15 minutes. Serve hot.

VEGETARIAN (LO HAN ZHAI) CASSEROLE
羅漢齋

Serves 4–6.

Preparation & cooking time: 30–35 mins.

Also known as 'Buddha's Delight', the original recipe uses no less than eighteen different items to represent the eighteen Buddhas (*Lo Han* being the Chinese name for Buddha). But nowadays the use of anything between six to eight items is the usual practice.

5g ($^1/_8$oz) dried black fungus (wood ears), see Glossary
300ml ($^1/_2$ pint) seasoned oil (see page 44)
1 cake bean-curd, cut into 16 small pieces
115g (4oz) Chinese leaves, cut into small pieces
1 small carrot, cut diagonally into thin slices
50g (2oz) mange-tout, topped and tailed
85g (3oz) fresh bean sprouts, washed and drained
1 teaspoon salt
$^1/_2$ teaspoon soft brown sugar
85g (3oz) sliced bamboo shoots, rinsed and drained
85g (3oz) straw mushrooms, drained (see Glossary)
1 tablespoon light soy sauce or oyster sauce
about 2–3 tablespoons stock (see page 45)
pinch of MSG (optional)
a few drops of sesame oil

Soak the black fungus in water for 10–20 minutes, rinse and drain well, discarding any hard bits.

Heat the oil in a preheated wok until hot, deep-fry the bean-curd pieces for about 2 minutes, remove and drain. Pour off the excess oil, leaving about 3 tablespoons in the wok, stir-fry the Chinese leaves for about 1 minute, then add the carrot, mange-tout and bean sprouts with the salt and sugar, stir-fry for another minute or so, then transfer the whole lot into a casserole. Add the black fungus, bamboo shoots, straw mushrooms, soy sauce or oyster sauce and stock, blend well and bring to the boil, then reduce the heat and braise under cover for 5 minutes.

Uncover and add MSG (if using) and sesame oil, stir for a few times more and serve.

12
RICE, NOODLES & *DIM SUM*

Rice has always been the staple food for the Chinese people south of the Yangtze River, while people in the north had to rely more on wheat products for their everyday meals.

As mentioned on page 33, the Chinese word *fan* covers all the staples (rice and wheat products, which includes noodles, pancakes and dumplings, etc). In everyday usage, the Chinese word for 'rice' and 'meal' are the same – just as in English the word 'bread' is used in 'the breadwinner' or 'give us our daily bread'.

Plain boiled or steamed rice is served for everyday meals, while fried rice and noodles (fried or in soup) should only be served on their own as a light meal or snack, apart from on special occasions, such as banquets and dinner parties.

BOILED RICE
白飯

Serves 4.

Preparation & cooking time: about 20–25 mins.

Use long grain or patna rice; or better still, try Fragrant Rice from Thailand.

225g (8oz) rice
200ml (¹/₃ pint) cold water
pinch of salt
¹/₂ teaspoon oil

Wash and rinse the rice just once. Place the rice in a saucepan and add the water so that there is no more than 2cm (²/₃") of water above the surface of the rice.

Bring to the boil, add salt and oil, then stir to prevent it sticking to the bottom of the pan.

Reduce the heat to very, very low and cook for 15–20 minutes under cover. Remove from the heat and let stand for 10 minutes before fluffing up the rice with a fork or spoon before serving.

EGG FRIED RICE
蛋炒飯

Serves 4.

Preparation & cooking time: about 5–10 mins.

The rice should be cold before frying.

3 eggs
1 teaspoon salt
2–3 tablespoons oil
450g (1lb) boiled rice
50g (2oz) peas
pinch of MSG (optional)

Lightly beat the eggs with a pinch of the salt.

Heat the oil in a preheated wok, lightly scramble the eggs. Add the rice and stir to make sure that each grain of rice is separated, then add the remaining salt, peas and MSG (if using), blend well and serve.

SPECIAL (YANGCHOW) FRIED RICE
楊洲炒飯

Serves 4.

Preparation & cooking time: 25–30 mins.

Special Fried Rice (also known as Yangchow Fried Rice), is more elaborate than Egg Fried Rice, and almost a meal in itself.

50g (2oz) peeled and cooked prawns
50g (2oz) cooked meat, such as Char Siu (see page 100) or chicken, etc
50g (2oz) peas
3 eggs
1 teaspoon salt
1 tablespoon finely chopped spring onions
4 tablespoons seasoned oil (see page 44)
1 tablespoon light soy sauce
1 tablespoon Chinese rice wine
450g (1lb) boiled rice

Dry the prawns and cut the meat into small dice about the same size as the peas.

Lightly beat the eggs with a pinch of the salt and a few bits of the spring onions.

Heat about half of the oil in a preheated wok, stir-fry the peas, prawns and meat for about 1 minute, add the soy sauce and wine; remove and reserve.

Heat the remaining oil and lightly scramble the eggs. Add the rice and stir to make sure that each grain of rice is separated, then add the remaining salt, spring onions and the cooked ingredients (prawns, meat and peas). Blend well and serve hot.

ASSORTED MEATS AND RICE
什錦燴飯

Serves 4.

Preparation & cooking time: about 30–40 mins.

This is a very popular 'one-plate dish' served in Cantonese restaurants. The ingredients vary according to the chef's whims or seasonal availabilities.

115g (4oz) prepared squid (see page 82)
about 50g (2oz) each of fresh pork, chicken, kidney and liver
2 teaspoons thick cornflour paste (see page 40)
about 115g (4oz) each of cooked duck, crispy pork and Char Siu (see page 100)
175g (6oz) vegetables, such as Chinese leaves or mange-tout or French beans
3 tablespoons seasoned oil (see page 44)
$^1/_2$ teaspoon salt
$^1/_2$ teaspoon soft brown sugar
1 tablespoon light soy sauce
1 teaspoon Chinese rice wine (optional)
8–12 ready-made fish balls
about 4 tablespoons stock (see page 45)
a few drops of sesame oil
450g (1lb) boiled rice

Prepare the squid as for Deep-fried Squid on page 82. Cut the pork, kidney and liver into small thin slices, coat them with about half of the cornflour paste. Cut the cooked meats into small bite-size pieces. Prepare the vegetables by cutting the Chinese leaves into small pieces (top and tail the mange-tout or French beans, if using instead of Chinese leaves).

Heat the oil in a preheated wok, and stir-fry the vegetables for 1 minute, then add the raw meats and squid with the salt, sugar, soy sauce and wine, blend well and add the cooked meats and fish balls with the stock, bring to the boil and stir-braise for about 1 more minute. Finally, thicken the gravy with the remaining cornflour paste, garnish with sesame oil and serve on a bed of hot boiled rice.

NB This 'dressing' (meats with vegetables) can be served with either Chow Mein or Noodles in Soup.

CHINESE SAUSAGE AND CHICKEN RICE
臘腸蒸鷄飯

Serves 3–4.

Preparation & cooking time: 30–35 mins.

Traditionally, this dish is cooked in a small casserole for each individual serving. But there is no reason why you shouldn't use a big pot or saucepan and cook enough for three to four people.

225g (8oz) fillet of chicken breast and/or thigh meat
$^1/_4$ teaspoon salt
1 teaspoon Chinese rice wine
1 teaspoon thick cornflour paste (see page 40)
225g (8oz) long grain rice
3 Chinese pork sausages, cut into thin diagonal slices
1 tablespoon finely chopped spring onions to garnish

For the sauce:
2 tablespoons light soy sauce
1 tablespoon Chinese rice wine
$^1/_2$ teaspoon caster sugar
$^1/_2$ teaspoon finely chopped garlic (optional)
$^1/_2$ teaspoon finely chopped fresh ginger root
a few drops of sesame oil

Cut the chicken meat into small bite-size pieces, mix with the salt, wine and cornflour paste.

Cook the rice as for the 'Boiled Rice' on page 223 in a pot or casserole but without the salt and oil. When it starts to boil, give it a stir and lay the chicken pieces on top of the rice with the sausage slices on top of the chicken. Reduce the heat to very low, cover the pot again and cook for 15–20 minutes. (Do *not* uncover the pot during cooking.)

To serve: heat the sauce until nearly boiling, pour it over the sausage and chicken rice, garnish with the spring onions and serve hot.

SEAFOOD CHOW MEIN
三鮮炒麵

Serves 4.

Preparation & cooking time: 30–35 mins.

85–115g (3–4oz) cleaned squid (see page 82)
3–4 fresh scallops
85g (3oz) uncooked prawns
$^1/_2$ egg white
1 tablespoon thick cornflour paste (see page 40)
450g (1lb) fresh or 9 oz (250g) dried egg noodles
5–6 tablespoons seasoned oil (see page 44)
50–85g (2–3oz) mange-tout or French beans, topped and tailed
$^1/_2$ teaspoon salt
$^1/_2$ teaspoon soft brown sugar
1 tablespoon Chinese rice wine
2 tablespoons light soy sauce
2 spring onions, finely shredded
a few drops of sesame oil

Open up the squid and score the inside in a criss-cross pattern, then cut into pieces about the size of postage stamps. Soak the squid in a bowl of boiling water until all the pieces curl up; rinse in cold water and drain.

Cut each scallop into 3–4 slices. Shell and de-vein the prawns (see page 127) and cut each in half lengthways. Mix the scallops and prawns with the egg white and cornflour paste.

Cook the noodles in salted boiling water according to the instructions on the packet – 2–3 minutes for dried noodles, or 1 minute for fresh ones – then drain and rinse under cold water. Mix with a little of the oil.

Heat about 2–3 tablespoons oil in a preheated wok until hot, stir-fry the mange-tout or beans and seafood for about 2 minutes, add the salt, sugar, wine, half of the soy sauce and about half of the spring onions, blend well and add a little stock (see page 45) if necessary. Remove and keep warm as the 'dressing'.

Heat the remaining oil and stir-fry the noodles for 2–3 minutes with the remaining soy sauce; remove to a large serving dish, pour the 'dressing' on top, and garnish with sesame oil and the remaining spring onions. Serve hot.

CHICKEN/PORK CHOW MEIN
鶏／肉絲炒麵

Serves 4.

Preparation & cooking time: 25–30 mins.

This is a basic recipe. The meat and/or vegetables can be varied as you wish, only bear in mind the principle of cutting all ingredients into matching shapes and sizes for the same dish: in this case, all the ingredients should be cut into thin shreds like the noodles.

450g (1lb) fresh or 250g (9oz) dried egg noodles
4–5 tablespoons seasoned oil (see page 44)
225g (8oz) chicken breastmeat, or pork fillet
115g (4oz) French beans
115g (4oz) fresh bean sprouts
1 teaspoon salt
$1/2$ teaspoon soft brown sugar
1 tablespoon Chinese rice wine
2 tablespoons light soy sauce
2 spring onions, finely shredded
little stock (see page 45), if necessary
a few drops of sesame oil

Cook the noodles in salted boiling water according to the instructions on the packet, then drain and rinse under cold water. Mix with a little oil.

Thinly shred the meat; top and tail the beans.

Heat about 2–3 tablespoons oil in a preheated wok until hot, stir-fry the vegetables and meat for about 2 minutes, add the salt, sugar, wine, half of the soy sauce and about half of the spring onions, blend well and add a little stock if necessary. Remove and keep warm as the 'dressing'.

Heat the remaining oil and stir-fry the noodles for 2–3 minutes with the remaining soy sauce; remove to a large serving dish, pour the 'dressing' on top, and garnish with the sesame oil and the remaining spring onions. Serve hot or cold.

NOODLES IN SOUP
鷄絲湯麵

Serves 4.

Preparation & cooking time: 20–25 mins.

Noodles in soup (*tang mein*) are far more popular than Fried Noodles (*chow mein*) in China. This is a basic recipe; you can use different ingredients for the 'dressing' to suit your personal preference and taste.

225g (8oz) chicken breast or pork fillet (or ready cooked meat)
3–4 small dried Chinese mushrooms, soaked (see Glossary)
115g (4oz) sliced bamboo shoots, rinsed and drained
115g (4oz) spinach leaves, lettuce hearts, or Chinese leaves
2 spring onions, finely shredded
450g (1lb) fresh or 9 oz (250g) dried egg noodles
600ml (1 pint) stock (see page 45)
2 tablespoons seasoned oil (see page 44)
1 teaspoon salt
$1/2$ teaspoon soft brown sugar
1 tablespoon light soy sauce
2 teaspoons Chinese rice wine
a few drops of sesame oil

Thinly shred the meat. Squeeze dry the soaked mushrooms and discard any hard stalks. Thinly shred the mushrooms, bamboo shoots, vegetable and spring onions.

Cook the noodles in salted boiling water according to the instructions on the packet, then drain and rinse under cold water. Place in a serving bowl.

Bring the stock to the boil and pour over the noodles; keep warm.

Heat the oil in a pre-heated wok, add about half of the spring onions and all the meat, stir-fry for about 1 minute.

Now add the vegetables (mushrooms, bamboo shoots and greens), stir-fry for another minute. Add all the seasonings and blend well.

Pour the 'dressing' over the noodles, garnish with the remaining spring onions and serve.

WANTONS IN SOUP
雲吞湯

Serves 4.

Preparation & cooking time: 40–45 mins.

Served as a light meal (*Dim Sum* or snack).

170g (6oz) pork, not too lean, coarsely chopped
50g (2oz) peeled prawns, finely minced
1 teaspoon soft brown sugar
1 tablespoon Chinese rice wine
1 tablespoon light soy sauce
1 teaspoon finely chopped spring onions
1 teaspoon finely chopped fresh ginger root
32 ready-made Wanton skins
about 750ml (1¼ pints) stock (see page 45)
1 tablespoon light soy sauce (for seasoning)
finely chopped spring onions to garnish

Mix the pork and prawns with the sugar, wine, soy sauce, spring onions and ginger. Blend well and leave to stand for 25–30 minutes.

Place about 1 teaspoon filling at the centre of a Wanton skin. Wet with water, fold the Wanton over and join the edges, pressing to seal them. Pull out the edges to form a floral shape.

Bring the stock to a rolling boil, and cook for 4–5 minutes. Season, garnish, then serve.

Fig. 28. Preparing the Wantons.

SINGAPORE FRIED NOODLES
星洲炒米粉

Serves 4.

Preparation & cooking time: 20–25 mins.

Also known as 'Rice Sticks', rice noodles or vermicelli are very popular in southern China, where they are interchangeable with noodles made from wheat flour.

275–350g (10–12oz) rice vermicelli or noodles
1 tablespoon dried shrimps, soaked
115g (4oz) cooked pork, chicken or Char Siu (see page 100), shredded
4 tablespoons seasoned oil (see page 44)
1 medium onion, thinly shredded
115g (4oz) fresh bean sprouts
1 teaspoon salt
1 tablespoon mild curry powder
2 tablespoons light soy sauce
1–2 spring onions, thinly shredded
1–2 green or red hot chillies, seeded and finely shredded*

Soak the rice noodles in hot water for 5–10 minutes, rinse in cold water and drain.

Drain the dried shrimps. Thinly shred the meat or Char Siu.

Heat about 2 tablespoons oil in a preheated wok, stir-fry the onion and bean sprouts with the meat and shrimps for about 1 minute, then add the noodles with the salt, curry powder and soy sauce, blend well; stir-fry for another minute, now add the spring onions and chillies, stir and toss for a few times. Serve hot.

*NB Always handle fresh hot chillies with great care. See page 52.

CRISPY SPRING ROLLS
炸春卷

Makes 20 rolls.

Preparation & cooking time: 40–45 mins. & cooling time.

This is a vegetarian recipe. For a non-vegetarian version, just replace the mushrooms with chicken or pork, and the carrot with prawns.

Frozen spring roll skins are readily available from Oriental stores; once defrosted, they should be kept under a damp cloth.

225g (8oz) fresh bean sprouts
1 medium carrot
115g (4oz) sliced bamboo shoots, rinsed and drained
115g (4oz) white mushrooms
4–5 spring onions, thinly shredded
3–4 tablespoons seasoned oil (see page 44)
1 teaspoon salt
$^1/_2$ teaspoon soft brown sugar
1 tablespoon light soy sauce
1 tablespoon Chinese rice wine
pinch of MSG (optional)
1 packet of 20 spring roll skins, defrosted
1 tablespoon plain flour paste
dry plain flour for dusting
oil for deep-frying

Wash and drain the bean sprouts. Cut the vegetables into fine shreds roughly the same size as the bean sprouts.

Heat the oil and stir-fry the vegetables for about 1 minute; add the salt, sugar, soy sauce and wine, continue stirring for another minute; add the MSG (if using), remove and drain off the excess liquid, then leave to cool for at least 1 hour.

To make the spring rolls: place about 2 tablespoons of the vegetables a little under half way down a sheet of the skin, and shape it into a 'sausage' (fig. 29a). Lift the lower flap over the filling and roll once (fig. 29b).

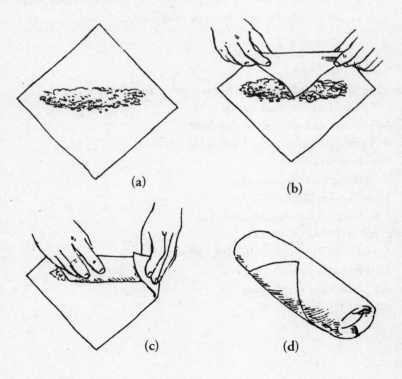

(a)

(b)

(c)

(d)

Fig. 29. Making the spring rolls.

Fold in both ends and roll once more (fig. 29c). Brush the remaining edge with a little flour paste and roll into a neat package (fig. 29d). Lightly dust a tray with dry flour and place the spring rolls on it with the flap-side down.

To cook: Heat the oil in a wok or deep-fryer until hot (180°C/350°F), then reduce the heat to 160°C/325°F and deep-fry the spring rolls in batches (say 3–4 at a time) for 2–3 minutes or until golden and crispy. Remove and drain.

Serve hot with a dip such as light soy sauce, rice vinegar, chilli sauce, or Spicy Salt and Pepper (see page 83).

NB Uncooked spring rolls can be kept in the refrigerator for 2–3 days; or they can be frozen for up to 12 months and then cooked from frozen.

CHOW MEIN (FRIED NOODLES)
净炒麵

Serves 4.

Preparation & cooking time: 10–15 mins.

This is a basic recipe for 'Plain Chow Mein'. For best results, use fresh egg noodles rather than dried ones.

450g (1lb) fresh, or 250g (9oz) dried egg noodles
3–4 tablespoons seasoned oil (see page 44)
1 small onion, finely shredded
115g (4oz) fresh bean sprouts
1–2 spring onions, finely shredded
2 tablespoons light soy sauce
pinch of MSG (optional)
a few drops of sesame oil

Cook the dried noodles in salted boiling water according to the instructions on the packet (usually no more than 2–3 minutes), then drain and rinse in cold water; drain again and mix with a little oil. Fresh noodles require far less cooking time – just soak in boiling water for 1 minute, then rinse in cold water and drain; mix with a little of the oil.

Heat the remaining oil in a preheated wok, stir-fry the onion for about 30 seconds, then add the bean sprouts, noodles and spring onions, stir and toss for 1 more minute or so; add the soy sauce and MSG (if using), blend well. Finally add the sesame oil and serve.

PORK DUMPLINGS (JIAO ZI)
餃子

To make about 80–90 dumplings.

Preparation & cooking time: about 1–1¹/₂ hours.

These dumplings are most versatile: they make a good starter when shallow-fried (see page 246) or steamed; they can also be served on their own as a snack; or as a complete meal when poached in large quantities – say 12–16 per person.

The pork can be replaced with lamb or beef; and for a vegetarian version, the meat can be substituted with dried Chinese mushrooms and bamboo shoots or carrots.

For the dough:
450g (1lb) plain flour
about 450ml (³/₄ pint) water
dry flour for dusting

For the filling:
450g (1lb) Chinese leaves or white cabbage
450g (1lb) minced pork
1 tablespoon finely chopped spring onions
1 teaspoon finely chopped fresh ginger root
2 teaspoons salt
1 teaspoon granulated sugar
2 tablespoons light soy sauce
1 tablespoon Chinese rice wine
a pinch of MSG (optional)
2 teaspoons sesame oil

Sift the flour into a bowl, slowly pour in the water and mix to a firm dough. Knead until smooth and soft, then cover with a damp cloth and set aside for 25–30 minutes.

Blanch the cabbage leaves until soft. Drain and finely chop. Mix with the rest of the ingredients to make the filling.

To make the dumplings: Lightly dust a work surface with dry flour, knead and roll the dough into a long sausage about 2.5cm (1") in diameter.

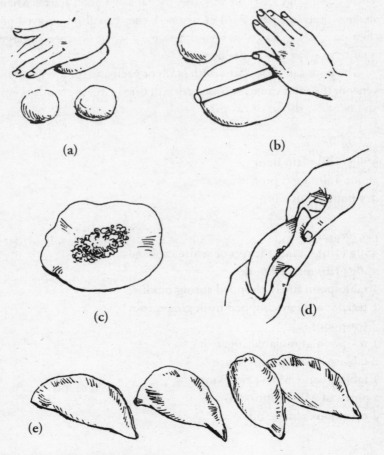

Fig. 30. Making the dumplings.

Cut the 'sausage' into about 80–90 small pieces; flatten each piece with the palm of your hand (fig. 30a). Use a rolling pin to roll out each piece into a thin pancake about 6cm (2.5") in diameter (fig. 30b).

Place about 1¹/₂ tablespoons filling in the centre of each pancake (fig. 30c). Fold it into a half-moon shaped pouch (fig. 30d), and pinch the edges firmly so that the dumpling is tightly sealed (fig. 30e). Place the dumplings on a tray lightly dusted with dry flour and cover with a damp cloth until ready for cooking.

Any uncooked dumplings should be frozen rather than just refrigerated – they can be kept in the freezer for up to six months or more, and can be cooked from frozen.

NB If you don't want to (or don't have the time to) make your own dumplings, frozen ready-made pork dumplings are widely available in most Chinese provision stores – in fact, most Chinese restaurants get their supplies from manufacturers who make the dumplings by machine.

To cook: The simplest way is by poaching or steaming:

POACHING: Bring about 900ml (1¹/₂ pints) water to a rolling boil, drop in about 20 dumplings, one by one, stirring gently with chopsticks to prevent them sticking together. Cover and bring back to the boil.

Uncover and add about 50ml (2fl oz) cold water, then bring back to the boil once more (uncovered). Repeat this process twice more. Remove and drain, serve with dip sauce 1 or 2 (see page 246).

STEAMING: Place the dumplings on a bed of lettuce leaves on the rack of a bamboo steamer and steam for 10–12 minutes on high heat. Serve with dip sauce 1 or 2 (see page 246).

GRILLED (SHALLOW-FRIED) PORK DUMPLINGS
鍋貼

Grilled or shallow-fried dumplings are also known as *kuotai* or 'pot-sticker' – they are crispy on the base, soft on top and juicy inside.

Make the dumplings as per page 243.

Heat about 3 tablespoons oil in a wok or frying-pan. When hot, tilt the pan so that the surface is evenly coated in oil.

Arrange the dumplings neatly in rows over the surface and fry over medium heat for 2–3 minutes, or until the base of each dumpling is browned.

Pour about 150ml (¼ pint) hot water down the side of the pan. Cover and increase the heat to high, and cook until almost all the water has evaporated.

Uncover and continue to cook until all the water is evaporated. Turn off the heat, and use a fish slice or spatula gently to loosen the dumplings from the bottom of the pan. Serve hot with dip sauce 1.

DIP SAUCE 1
2 tablespoons finely shredded fresh ginger root
3 tablespoons rice vinegar
2 tablespoons light soy sauce

DIP SAUCE 2
2 tablespoons red chilli oil
1 tablespoon light soy sauce
1 teaspoon finely chopped garlic
1 tablespoon finely chopped spring onions

13

DESSERTS

Almond Curd with Fruit Cocktail, page 248
Chinese Fruit Salad, page 249
Red Bean Paste Pancake, page 250
Toffee Apple/Banana, page 252

The Chinese seldom conclude an everyday meal with a dessert, hence the very limited range for this section. In China most sweet dishes are served either as a snack in between meals, or, on special occasions, served between courses to cleanse the palate, in the same manner as a sorbet.

ALMOND CURD WITH FRUIT COCKTAIL
杏仁豆腐

Serves 4.

Preparation & cooking time: about 20 mins & cooling time.

Gelatine powder can be used if you find it too difficult to track down agar-agar or isinglass.

about 10g (^{1}/$_4$oz) agar-agar or isinglass
300ml (^{1}/$_2$ pint) water
4 tablespoons granulated or caster sugar
300ml (^{1}/$_2$ pint) milk
1 teaspoon almond essence
canned mixed fruit cocktail with syrup

Dissolve the agar-agar or isinglass in water over very gentle heat – this will take about 10 minutes. Then add the sugar and milk with the almond essence, mix well and pour the mixture into a large serving bowl. When cool, refrigerate for 3–4 hours to chill and set.

To serve, cut the curd into sugar-lump size cubes, pour the fruit cocktail with syrup over it.

CHINESE FRUIT SALAD
什錦菓品

Serves 4–6.

Preparation time: 20–25 mins & chilling time.

Chilled fruit (fresh or canned) is most refreshing when served at the end of a big meal, particularly if it is beautifully presented.

115g (4oz) rock candy or crystal sugar (optional)
300ml (¹/₂ pint) water (optional)
1 small water melon or a large honeydew melon
4–5 different fresh and canned fruits, such as lychees, kiwi fruit, pineapple, pears, grapes, cherries, tangerines, banana, peaches, mango and papaya, etc
crushed ice to serve

If no canned fruit with syrup is used, dissolve the rock candy in the water over gentle heat, then leave to cool.

Slice off about 2.5cm (1") off the top of a melon and scoop out the flesh, discarding the seeds; cut the flesh into small chunks. Prepare other fresh fruits by cutting them into small chunks too.

Fill the melon shell with fruits and the syrup. Cover with clingfilm and chill in the refrigerator for 2–3 hours.

To serve, place the melon on a bed of crushed ice.

RED BEAN PASTE PANCAKE
豆沙鍋餅

Serves 4.

Preparation & cooking time: 10–15 mins if using ready-made pancakes.

Use ready-made 'Duck Pancakes' for this dish, or make them by following the recipe on page 106.

8 'Duck Pancakes' (see page 106)
about 8 tablespoons sweetened red bean paste
2 tablespoons vegetable oil
granulated or caster sugar to garnish

Spread about 1 tablespoon red bean paste evenly over about 85%–90% of the surface of a pancake (fig. 31a). Roll the pancake over three or four times (fig. 31b) to form a flattened roll (fig. 31c).

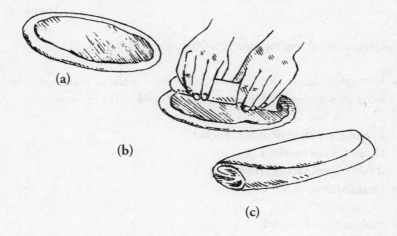

(a)

(b)

(c)

Fig. 31. Making the rolls.

To cook: Heat the oil in a preheated wok or frying-pan, then shallow-fry the pancake rolls until golden brown on both sides. Cut each roll into 3–4 pieces, garnish with sugar and serve hot.

TOFFEE APPLE/BANANA
拔絲蘋菓／香蕉

Serves 4.

Preparation & cooking time: 15–20 mins.

Apart from apple and banana, other fruits such as pineapple and water chestnuts can be prepared and cooked in the same way.

3 eating apples/4 bananas, peeled
115g (4oz) plain flour
about 100ml (4fl oz) cold water
1 egg, beaten
oil for deep-frying
1 tablespoon fresh oil
115g (4oz) granulated or caster sugar
1 teaspoon white sesame seeds (optional)

Cut the apples/bananas into about 16 pieces. Dust the pieces with a little dry flour.

Sift the remaining flour into a mixing bowl, slowly add the water to make a smooth paste, then add the beaten egg, blend well to make a batter.

Dip the apple/banana pieces in the batter and deep-fry in hot oil for about 3 minutes or until golden; remove and drain.

Heat the fresh oil in a preheated wok, add the sugar, stir continuously until the sugar is caramelized, then quickly add the fruit pieces, blending well so that each piece is coated with the 'toffee', and add the sesame seeds (if using). Dip the pieces in cold water to harden before serving.

14

MENU PLANNING & WHAT TO DRINK WITH CHINESE FOOD

One of the most frequently asked questions at my cookery classes is, 'How can I serve different dishes at the same time and keep them all hot?'

The answer or secret is, of course, to plan your menu carefully.

As explained on page 15 of the Introduction, four or even six different items can appear simultaneously, all piping hot, on your table in a restaurant because of the facilities and resources provided in a professional kitchen, which are almost impossible to match at home. However, all is not lost when cooking in your own home. What you must remember is that, unless you want to spend the entire duration of the meal in the kitchen yourself, you should never have more than two (or three at the very most) dishes that require last minute cooking. Fortunately, as you must have noticed, most Chinese dishes require far more preparation time than actual cooking time.

The first point to take into consideration when planning a menu is that a Chinese meal does not follow the conventional Western serving order of soup, fish, poultry, meat and dessert. (Perhaps most Westerners are confused and bewildered when faced with a long Chinese menu, not only because of the unfamiliar names of the dishes, but also because the dishes are arranged under headings of the conventional Western categories, which are not really helpful to the layman when selecting dishes to make up an authentic Chinese meal.)

One obstacle which faces you when planning your menu is that (as I mentioned briefly in the Foreword) it is often difficult to get the exact dish you require in a restaurant due to the inaccurate and misleading descriptions of Chinese cooking terms and dish names which have been passed down through the years.

Then there is the problem of seeking help from the waiters or waitresses. It is a fact that a great number of the staff in most Chinese restaurants have never had formal training in service, let alone a good command of English. Furthermore, they are sometimes arrogant and rude-mannered, so you are not likely to get much help from them when seeking advice on menu planning.

It's true that almost every restaurant has a set menu for two or more persons, but I am sorry to say that a great majority of these menus have been put together purely for the 'foreigners' (i.e. non-Chinese), without much regard to the structure of a genuine Chinese meal. I shall explain:

The standard set menu always starts with a soup (usually Sweetcorn and Crabmeat/Chicken, Hot and Sour, or Wanton; it is sometimes followed by one or two 'starters' such as Spare-ribs, Spring Rolls, Crispy Seaweed and Sesame Prawn Toasts, etc; then there will be a number of stir-fried dishes which invariably will include the ubiquitous Sweet and Sour Pork or whatever, served almost always with Fried Rice; ending up with a dessert.

So what's wrong with that, you may wonder, for these are all the most popular dishes people enjoy eating, and probably these are the very dishes you would most like to reproduce at home yourself.

Now let's analyse both the content of such a menu, and the practicality of reproducing it at home.

To start with, the Sweetcorn and Crabmeat/Chicken Soup is not actually Chinese – like Chop Suey, it is American in origin – and although both the Hot and Sour and Wanton Soups are the genuine article, all three are really too 'heavy' for a first course.

In China, soup is never served at the beginning of a meal. The customary practice is to serve a light, simply made soup throughout the meal: it is meant to act as a lubricant to help wash down the bulky and savoury foods, since we do not have the habit of drinking water (nor tea for that matter – more details later) with an everyday meal. Only on special or formal occasions, would soup be served as a separate course. Even then, it would only be served at the end of the meal, or between the starter and main courses, in order to cleanse the palate for the next course, so for that reason, the soup should always be very light and not too strongly flavoured or seasoned.

Then there is the question of serving a piping hot soup as the very first course at home – what are you going to do with the rest of the meal? Do you intend to spend a considerable time in the kitchen to cook the next course, while the guests or the family are kept waiting for you to produce the food?

If you have recovered from the initial shock, I have more news for you. Avoid serving hot starters that require last minute cooking at home – for the same reasons as serving hot soup at the beginning of a meal – it's just too much hard work for the cook. There are exceptions to the rule of course: for instance, Crispy 'Seaweed' or 'Butterfly' Prawns are just two of the dishes which can 'hold' for quite a long time without losing too much flavour or crispiness.

As for the main course of mostly stir-fried or quick-braised dishes, which definitely need to be cooked just before serving, careful planning is essential for the home kitchen. The most important point is to limit the number of dishes to no more than two or three at the very most, otherwise you will have to serve the dishes one by one instead of simultaneously.

Plain rice rather than fried rice should be served with the main course. In China, fried rice (and chow mein) are never served with a main meal, except at a banquet when they become part of the *dim sum* (snacks) course, which consists of both savoury and sweet items, at the end of a menu as desserts.

Lastly, try not to have a hot dessert course for your Chinese meal at home, unless you serve such traditional items like Roly-Poly or a fruit crumble, neither of which requires last minute cooking. Otherwise just serve a cold dessert which can be prepared well in advance.

Menu Planning

As I explained in the Introduction (page 13), the aim of a Chinese meal is **harmony** and **variety** – in colour, aroma, flavour and texture – both in a single dish *and* in a course of dishes. This can only be achieved by using different ingredients and various cooking methods.

You must remember that not only is there a distinctive style of *cooking* Chinese food, but also there is an art in *eating* Chinese food – which applies both to the ordering in a restaurant, and to the cooking at home.

An everyday, informal Chinese meal is essentially a hot buffet with a number of dishes (including soup) served on the table at the same time. Even at a formal banquet or dinner party, the dishes are served in groups rather than singly. This is particularly important to remember when entertaining at home.

In China, people generally eat in groups – as a family, or a group of friends. For that reason, almost all the recipes in this book are for a minimum of four. Now if you are cooking for just one or two people, obviously you only need to use about half or even less of the quantity. Another point to bear in mind is that we seldom serve just one dish for a main meal – even the 'one plate' light lunch served in the fast food eateries always consists of at least three different ingredients (meat, vegetable and rice or noodles), and you may have noticed that very often an expatriate will order a big bowl of Wanton and/or noodle soup to go with it.

Apart from the 'snack' lunch, the Chinese never serve an individual dish to each person – everyone shares the dishes on the table, in that way you can enjoy a variety of dishes.

So the general rule is to have one more dish than there are people: three dishes for two, five for four and so on (including rice and perhaps soup). But if you are entertaining a big party, say 8–10 people, then 6–8 dishes should be sufficient, otherwise it would become too lavish, and too much hard work for the cook.

With that in mind, here are a few suggested menus for all occasions:

SAMPLE MENU FOR 2–3 PEOPLE
Stir-fried prawns/chicken/meat with vegetables
A Steamed/Braised dish
Fish Balls & Watercress/Chicken & Mushroom Soup (optional)
Boiled Rice

The steamed or braised dish and rice should be cooked first, since both the stir-fried dish and soup (if using) require last minute cooking. Instead of serving a steamed or braised dish and a soup (which is optional), why not serve a casserole (which has quite a lot of liquid anyway)? Since almost all the stir-fried dishes contain vegetable(s), there is no need to prepare a separate vegetable dish, thus saving you extra last minute cooking time.

SAMPLE MENU FOR 4–5 PEOPLE
A Cold Starter
1 or 2 Stir-fried dishes
A Steamed/Roasted/Braised dish
Soup (optional)
Boiled Rice

My remarks for the first sample menu apply to this one as well – try avoiding as much last minute cooking as possible.

SAMPLE MENU FOR 6–8 PEOPLE
1 or 2 Cold Starters
1 Deep-fried or Roasted dish
2 Stir-fried dishes
A Steamed and a Braised dish or 2 Braised dishes
Boiled Rice
Dessert (optional)

As you can see, this menu again minimizes the number of dishes that require last minute cooking. Depending on the occasion or the appetites of the people, one or two dishes can easily be omitted from this menu.

SAMPLE MENU FOR 10–12 PEOPLE
2–3 or an assortment of 5–6 Cold Starters
1 Deep-fried and 1 Roasted Dish or 2 Deep-fried dishes
2 Stir-fried Dishes
2 Braised Dishes
Rice
Cold Dessert or Soup

If you are cooking for more than ten people, it would probably be a dinner party rather than an informal everyday meal, so I've separated the different courses into groupings. I'm afraid there is no way you, the cook, can be seated at the table throughout the meal, because the dishes have to be served course by course, not all together at the same time.

Now if you want to have a really big party for say 16–20 plus, I would recommend a buffet-style spread – with the dishes to be served hot, marked with an asterisk*:

SAMPLE BUFFET MENU FOR 16 OR MORE PEOPLE
'White-Cut' Chicken or Bang-Bang Chicken
'Smoked' Fish
'White-Cut' Pork
Pickled Cucumber
Soy-Braised Duck or Roast Duck Cantonese Style
'Butterfly' Prawns*
Barbecued Pork Spare-Ribs*
Braised Whole Fish or Steamed Fish with Ginger & Spring
Onions
Stir-fried Mixed Vegetables or Broccoli, Lettuce Hearts, etc
Fried Rice*
Chow Mein* or Singapore Fried Noodles*
Chinese Fruit Salad

Again, depending on the occasion and the appetites of the people, dishes can be omitted or added. The idea, as you know, is to have harmony and variety in colour, aroma, flavour and texture. In this case, the visual appeal must be supreme – the taste is very important of course, but what greets the eye when all the dishes are spread out on the table must be both pleasing and impressive.

What to Drink with Chinese Food

Contrary to common belief in the West, tea is seldom served at mealtimes in China. It is true that tea is the most popular beverage of most Chinese, but it is usually drunk before or after, but not during, a meal, not even at breakfast. When we talk of taking morning tea, we really mean 'elevenses' – i.e. after breakfast, but before the midday lunch.

You may well wonder at this point why most people (including the expatriates – but *not* this one, I hasten to add) seem always to be drinking pots of tea with their meals in a Chinese restaurant. I'll explain.

I mentioned in the Initial Preparation (page 33) the differences of *fan* and *cai* in Chinese food. What I didn't elaborate at that stage is the fact that cai dishes are divided into either *jiu-cai* ('wine-dishes') – i.e. food to be eaten with wine; or *fan-cai* ('rice-dishes') – i.e. food to be eaten with rice or other grains.

The 'wine-dishes' are the cold starters, roasted and deep-fried dishes, as well as some stir-fried dishes; while 'rice-dishes' are braised and steamed dishes, also casseroles and dishes that contain a certain amount of gravy, including some of the stir-fried dishes.

'Wine-dishes' are usually (but not always) served in restaurants rather than in homes, except on special occasions or when entertaining. For everyday lunches or suppers, 'rice-dishes' are usually served with a soup, not as a separate course, but throughout the meal, and never with tea.

But I still have not explained why people drink tea with their meals in Chinese restaurants in the West. Please bear with me just a little longer.

We have basically four categories of restaurants or eateries in China: large establishments that cater for big banquets as well as small informal parties; restaurants without banqueting facilities but which offer food of high quality; then there are bistro-style small eateries with a limited menu; finally, the tea-houses and mess-halls or canteens.

When you go to any of these places, you will be offered tea automatically on arrival. With the exception of the 'tea-house', the tea is not meant to go with the meal, but to be an *aperitif* while you wait for the food.

However, when it comes to visiting a tea-house (the nearest equivalent to a café or snack bar), the main objective is to drink tea, usually without any food (although it is possible to order a snack or light meal in the form of dumplings, noodles or Wantons and so on, in some of these establishments). But the Cantonese have developed 'tea and snacks' into a fine art known as *dim sum*, literally meaning 'dot on the heart' i.e. a snack or refreshment, not a proper meal.

When the first wave of Chinese restaurants opened in the West, they were run by people who had migrated from the southern region of China (Canton and Fujian). Very few of these establishments employed really good chefs, or properly trained waiting staff, let alone a wine waiter or *sommelier*, with the result that when you dined out at a Chinese restaurant there was never anybody with a deep understanding of Chinese food and wine to advise you.

This situation did not improve following the rapid expansion of Chinese restaurants in Britain in the mid-1960s. The standard of cooking certainly went up, but the high quality of food was not matched by the service, and the 'tea-house' mentality prevailed even in the so-called Peking/Sichuan restaurants which is why people drink tea in them.

I would also like to dispel the misconception, commonly held in the West, that Chinese food and wine do not go well together. This is of course nonsense.

Some people regard Chinese food as too 'spicy' for wine – but have they ever stopped to think about the richness of the Mediterranean food which is always served with wine? I am thinking of the French herbs such as *bouquet garni* not to mention the onions, garlic, tomatoes, peppers and chillies, etc, widely used in French, Italian and Spanish cooking. Then there are those who recommend a white wine for *all* Chinese food – obviously that cannot be right either, unless you happen to dislike drinking red wine.

I think all these 'misguided' opinions are partly caused by the unorthodox way the Chinese serve their food, which completely throws into confusion the Western convention (a rather tenuous one, I believe) of matching white wine with fish and white meat, and red wine with red meat and cheese.

But as I have stated earlier, a Chinese meal is planned according to a carefully worked out programme based on the *yin-yang* principle – harmony and contrast. So we may have red meat before white meat or fish, and what determines the serving order of dishes or courses is not so much the food itself, but rather the way it is prepared and cooked. Thus we have lightly seasoned dishes (some cold, some hot, and mostly dry with a little sauce perhaps, but never gravy) as starters; these are followed by stir-fried and/or quick-braised dishes, again not strongly flavoured nor 'heavy' with sauce or gravy, for all the dishes from these two courses are known as *shao-cai* ('little dishes') or *jiu-cai* ('wine-dishes'). Next, depending on the occasion or the size of the party, we have what is known as the principal dish such as Peking Duck, Aromatic and Crispy Duck, or Lobster, etc., which is followed by the main course of long-braised and steamed dishes served with rice. They are called *da-cai* ('big dishes') or *fan-cai* ('rice-dishes'), usually strongly seasoned and 'heavy' with sauce or gravy.

Choosing wine or wines for a menu like this should never be a big problem – the secret is not to try to match a particular wine with an individual dish, but rather to look for a wine which will bring harmony to a course of different dishes, or be able to complete an overall equilibrium, since each Chinese dish or course of dishes is so carefully balanced in accordance with the principle of a harmonious blending of colour, aroma, flavour and texture.

So the only point we have to observe here is that, as a rule, light wines (usually white or rosé, but also some reds) should be served before full-bodied and weighty wines (nearly always red). Another point to remember is that if you are going to serve two or three wines of similar nature, then always start with the younger vintage before serving an older and matured one. In other words, always save the best bottle until last.

Although I am not a 'beer man', there is no reason why you should not drink beer or lager with Chinese food if you prefer beer to wine – lots of people do so in China. I certainly would not advocate the fairly wide Chinese practice of drinking Cognac with their food! Much as I adore French Cognac, I drink it only as a *digestif* after the meal, never with it.

After a good Chinese meal, nothing is more refreshing than a large pot of hot Jasmine tea – clear, pale and scented, but *without* sugar or milk.

There is a very wide range of varieties of tea in China, but basically they are divided into five main groups: **Black**, **Green**, **Oolong**, **Scented**, and **Brick**.

Black teas are prepared using the normal process of fermentation and they have a strong flavour and a honey-like aroma. The Chinese call them 'red' teas because of the colour of the brewed tea.

Green teas are dried and roasted (like the black) but not fermented, consequently they are lighter and more subtly flavoured.

Oolong (which means 'black dragon' in Chinese) tea, which is only semi-fermented, is a special product of Fujian province in southeast China (and also in Taiwan). Oolong teas are particularly popular in south China and among expatriate Chinese all over the world.

Scented teas are prepared by adding dried flower petals, such as jasmine, magnolia and rose, to high quality green tea. Scented teas are more popular overseas than in China.

Brick teas are essentially black teas, fermented, roasted and dried, but then compressed into oblong 'bricks'. They can be stored for a long time without losing their flavour.

In China, true tea connoisseurs are very particular about the origin, age, preparation and storage of their favourite brew. They also pay close attention not only to the quality and temperature of the water, but also the fire wood, the kettle, the teapot and cups used in the brewing and serving. A good tea is judged by its colour, aroma and flavour. It should be sipped and appreciated on its own without any real food – the most common accompaniment of tea in China is a dish of melon seeds, which can hardly be called 'food'.

GLOSSARY

Agar-agar Also known as **Isinglass** (*kanten* in Japanese).
A product of seaweed, sold dried in paper-thin strands or powdered
form. Gelatine may be substituted.

Baby corn cobs
Baby corn cobs have a wonderfully sweet fragrance and flavour, and
an irresistible texture. Available both fresh and canned.

Bamboo shoots
Available in cans only. Once opened, the contents may be kept in
fresh water in a covered jar for up to a week in the refrigerator. Try
to get *Winter bamboo shoots*, which have a 'sweeter' flavour and
firmer texture. Ready sliced bamboo shoots are also available.

Bean-curd (tofu)
This custard-like preparation of puréed and pressed soya beans is
exceptionally high in protein. It is usually sold in cakes about 7.5cm
(3") square and 2.5cm (1") thick in Oriental and health food stores.
Will keep for a few days if submerged in water in a container and
placed in the refrigerator.

Bean sprouts
Fresh bean sprouts, from mung or soya beans, are widely available
from Oriental stores and all supermarkets. They can be kept in the
refrigerator for two to three days.

Black bean sauce
Salted black beans crushed and mixed with flour and spices (such as
ginger, garlic or chilli, etc) to make a thickish paste. Sold in jars or
cans. Once opened, it should be kept in the refrigerator.

Chilli bean sauce

Fermented bean paste mixed with hot chilli and other seasonings. Sold in jars. Some are quite mild, but some are very hot. You will have to try out the various brands yourself to see which one is to your taste.

Chilli oil

Made from dried red chillies, garlic, onions, salt and vegetable oil. Extremely hot. Used only as a dip at the table rather than for cooking in the kitchen.

Chilli sauce

Very hot sauce made from chillies, vinegar, sugar and salt. Usually sold in bottles. Should be used sparingly in cooking or as a dip.

Chinese leaves

Also known as **Chinese cabbage**. The two most widely available varieties are sold in supermarkets and green groceries. The most commonly seen one has a pale green colour and tightly wrapped elongated head; about two-thirds of the cabbage is stem which has a crunchy texture. The other variety has a shorter and fatter head with curlier, pale yellow or green leaves; also with a white stem.

Coriander

Fresh coriander leaves, also known as Chinese parsley or *cilantro*, are widely used in Chinese cooking as a garnish.

Dried Chinese mushrooms (Shiitake)

Highly fragrant dried mushrooms sold in plastic bags; they are not cheap, but a small amount will go a long way, and they will keep indefinitely in an airtight jar. Soak them in warm water for 20–30 minutes (or in cold water for at least 1 hour), squeeze dry and discard the hard stalks before use.

Egg noodles
There are many varieties of noodles in China – ranging from flat, broad ribbons to long and narrow strands. Both dried and fresh noodles are available in the West.

Five-spice powder
A mixture of star anise, fennel seeds, cloves, cinnamon bark and Sichuan pepper. It is highly piquant, so should be used very sparingly. It will keep in an airtight container indefinitely.

Ginger root
Fresh ginger root, sold by weight, should be peeled and sliced, finely chopped or shredded before use. It will keep for weeks in a dry, cool place. Dried ginger powder is no substitute.

Ground fried fish
Available in 200g (7oz) vacuum packed tins; once opened, it should keep for several months in a dry and cool place.

Hoi Sin sauce
Also known as **barbecue sauce**. Made from soy beans, sugar, flour, vinegar, salt, garlic, chilli and sesame seed oil. Sold in cans or jars, it will keep in the refrigerator for several months.

Oyster sauce
A thickish sauce used as a flavouring in Cantonese cooking. Sold in bottles, it will keep in the refrigerator for months.

Plum sauce
Plum sauce has a unique fruity flavour – a sweet and sour sauce with a difference.

Prawns
In Britain, prawns are usually sold ready cooked, either in their shells or peeled; these are not really suitable for Chinese cooking. Try to get

the uncooked variety known as king or tiger prawns, frozen when fresh, either in their shells and headless, or shelled. They should always be thoroughly defrosted and de-veined before use (see page 127).

Red bean paste
This reddish-brown paste is made from puréed red beans and crystallized sugar. Sold in cans, the leftover contents should be transferred to a covered container and will keep in the refrigerator for several months.

Rice vinegar
There are two basic types of rice vinegar: Red Vinegar is made from fermented rice and has a distinctive dark colour and depth of flavour; White Vinegar is stronger in flavour as it is distilled from rice. In some of the recipes I haven't specified which type to use as you can use either in them.

Rice wine
Chinese rice wine, made from glutinous rice, is also known as 'Yellow wine' (*Huang jiu* or *chiew* in Chinese), because of its golden amber colour. The best variety is called **Shao Hsing** or **Shaoxing** from southeast China. A good dry or medium sherry can be an acceptable substitute.

Rock candy or sugar
Made with a combination of cane sugar and honey. It adds a special sheen to foods that have been stewed with it. Crystal sugar can be a substitute.

Salted black beans
Very salty and pungent! Sold in plastic bags, jars or cans; should be crushed with water or wine before use. Will keep almost indefinitely in a covered jar.

Satay sauce
Made from crushed peanut and flavoured with soy sauce, chilli, shallot, sugar, vinegar and garlic, this highly aromatic and piquant sauce is used as a dip rather than for cooking.

Sesame oil
Sold in bottles and widely used in China as a garnish rather than for cooking. The refined yellow sesame oil sold in Middle Eastern stores is not so aromatic, has less flavour and therefore is not a substitute.

Sichuan peppercorns
Also known as *farchiew*, they are wild red peppers from Sichuan. More aromatic but less hot than either white or black peppers, they do give a quite unique flavour to the food.

Soy sauce
Sold in bottles or cans, this most popular Chinese sauce is used both for cooking and at the table. *Light soy sauce* has more flavour than the sweeter *Dark soy sauce*, which gives the food a rich, reddish colour.

Straw mushrooms (*Voluariella volvacea*)
Grown on beds of rice straw, hence the name, straw mushrooms have a pleasant slippery texture, and a subtle taste. Canned straw mushrooms should be rinsed and drained after opening.

Szechwan preserved vegetables
The pickled mustard root is very hot and salty. Sold in cans, once opened, it should be stored in a tightly sealed jar in the refrigerator. It will keep for many months.

Wanton skins
Made from wheat flour, egg and water, these wafer-thin Wanton wrappers are sold in 7.5cm (3") squares from Oriental stores. They can be frozen, and will keep for up to six months.

Water chestnuts
Strictly speaking, water chestnuts do not belong to the chestnut family, they are the roots of a plant (*Heleocharis tuberosa*). Also known as *horse's hooves* in China on account of their appearance before the skin is peeled off. They are available fresh or in cans. Canned water chestnuts retain only part of the texture, and even less of the flavour, of fresh ones. Will keep for about a month in the refrigerator in a covered jar, changing the water every two or three days.

Wood ears also known as *Cloud ears*
They are dried black fungus (*Auricularia auricula*). Sold in plastic bags in Oriental stores, they should be soaked in cold or warm water for 20 minutes, then rinsed in fresh water before use. They have a crunchy texture and a mild but subtle flavour.

Yellow bean sauce
A thick paste made from salted, fermented yellow soya beans, crushed with flour and sugar. It is sold in cans or jars, and once the can is opened, the contents should be transferred to a screw-top jar. It will then keep in the refrigerator for months.

INDEX